New Directions for
Child and Adolescent
Development

William Damon
EDITOR-IN-CHIEF

Social and Self Processes Underlying Math and Science Achievement

Heather A. Bouchey
Cynthia E. Winston
EDITORS

Number 106 • Winter 2004
Jossey-Bass
San Francisco

SOCIAL AND SELF PROCESSES UNDERLYING MATH AND SCIENCE ACHIEVEMENT
Heather A. Bouchey, Cynthia E. Winston (eds.)
New Directions for Child and Adolescent Development, no. 106
William Damon, Editor-in-Chief

Microfilm copies of issues and articles are available in 16mm and 35mm, as well as microfiche in 105mm, through University Microfilms Inc., 300 North Zeeb Road, Ann Arbor, Michigan 48106-1346.

ISSN 1520-3247   electronic ISSN 1534-8687

NEW DIRECTIONS FOR CHILD AND ADOLESCENT DEVELOPMENT is part of The Jossey-Bass Education Series and is published quarterly by Wiley Subscription Services, Inc., a Wiley company, at Jossey-Bass, 989 Market Street, San Francisco, California 94103-1741. Periodicals postage paid at San Francisco, California, and at additional mailing offices. Postmaster: Send address changes to New Directions for Child and Adolescent Development, Jossey-Bass, 989 Market Street, San Francisco, CA 94103-1741.

New Directions for Child and Adolescent Development is indexed in Biosciences Information Service, Current Index to Journals in Education (ERIC), Psychological Abstracts, and Sociological Abstracts.

SUBSCRIPTIONS cost $90.00 for individuals and $205.00 for institutions, agencies, and libraries.

EDITORIAL CORRESPONDENCE should be sent to the Editor-in-Chief, William Damon, Stanford Center on Adolescence, Cypress Building C, Stanford University, Stanford, CA 94305.

Jossey-Bass Web address: www.josseybass.com

CONTENTS

EDITORS' NOTES

In general, America's students are not faring well in science and mathematics. By the eighth grade, students in the United States score below the international average and demonstrate lower performance in these courses than students in several other countries (Schmidt, McKnight, Cogan, Jakwerth, & Houang, 1999). Although the worrisome status of U.S. students in math and science is not a new problem facing this country, the ramifications of our international standing are far greater at this time than perhaps at any other in the history of the United States. Enhanced attainment and participation in science and mathematics fields are fundamental to the products, services, standard of living, and national security of the United States, particularly in the new globalized economy. Underscoring the importance of adolescents' motivation and success in mathematics and science, the American Association for the Advancement of Science cautioned that "what the future holds in store for individual human beings, the nation and the world largely depends on the wisdom with which humans use science, math, and technology" (AAAS, 1989).

With this current state of affairs in mind, we brought together a group of scholars whose work sheds light on how we may eventually maximize American adolescents' math and science achievement. It is well established in the motivation literature that both social and self processes play an important role in achievement motivation and academic performance (see Eccles, Wigfield, & Schiefele, 1998). However, the complex interplay of these factors has not been adequately examined to date. The chapters in this volume employ novel conceptual and empirical approaches to investigate how social and individual-level factors interact to effect successful math and science achievement. Each of the chapters is solidly grounded in theory and provides new insights concerning the integration of student-level and contextual influences.

As the earliest socializing agents in development, parents historically have been afforded central status as achievement socializers. In Chapter One, Janis E. Jacobs and Martha M. Bleeker extend previous work in the parenting arena by exploring specific mechanisms by which parents promote math and science achievement. They find an interesting pattern of gender differences, whereby parents purchase more math and science toys for sons than daughters but are more involved in daughters' math and science activities. In addition, parents' behaviors longitudinally predict their children's involvement and interest in math. By explicitly identifying and testing the effects of different behaviors, this work enhances our understanding of the important role of parents in the math and science domain.

The role of peers in promoting (or thwarting) academic achievement has recently captured scholars' attention (see Kindermann, McCollam, & Gibson, 1996; Ryan, 2001). In Chapter Two, Lisa M. Pettitt adds to this emerging literature by investigating the extent to which peer stereotypes regarding math and social domains change with pubertal development. She finds support for the "gender intensification" of peer socialization in each of these domains. This work clearly identifies the interplay of individual pubertal changes and social factors with respect to math and science achievement as an area ripe for further research.

To date, the majority of research on achievement socialization has focused on European American, middle-class samples. The final two chapters in this volume employ data from ethnic minority adolescents, an important addition to the literature on math and science achievement. In Chapter Three, Heather A. Bouchey adopts a symbolic interactionist perspective to explore both similarity and disparity in the ways that parents, teachers, and peers affect adolescents' math and science perceptions. By investigating the *same* processes for different social partners, this work advances our understanding of the interplay among different socializing agents on students' achievement. In addition, this research suggests that the classroom climate created by teachers and peers may be particularly "chilly" for Latino students.

Cynthia E. Winston and collaborators close this volume by laying out a provocative theoretical conceptualization for researching and understanding successful math and science achievement in African American adolescents. In Chapter Four, they argue that race is an important, yet understudied, *psychological* context influencing the formation of identity and concomitant achievement processes. The use of narrative theories of personality and discourse analysis are important theoretical frameworks for the central arguments advanced in this chapter; they are used to illustrate how race self complexity is incorporated into African American adolescents' achievement perceptions.

Collectively, the chapters in this volume present several advances and directions for future research on the development of math and science achievement. The work included here also raises many novel questions. We hope that the conceptual and empirical questions raised in the volume will stimulate more research that tackles the fascinating interplay among societal, interpersonal, and intrapersonal influences on math and science achievement.

Heather A. Bouchey
Cynthia E. Winston
Editors

References

American Association for the Advancement of Science. (1989). *Science for All Americans: Project 2061.* Washington, D.C.: American Association for the Advancement of Science.

Eccles, J. S., Wigfield, A., & Schiefele, U. (1998). Motivation to succeed. In W. Damon (Series Ed.) & N. Eisenberg (Vol. Ed.), *Handbook of child psychology: Vol. 3. Social, emotional, and personality development* (5th ed., pp. 1018–1095). New York: Wiley.

Kindermann, T. A., McCollam, T. L, & Gibson, E. (1996). Peer networks and students' classroom engagement during childhood and adolescence. In J. Juvonen & K. R. Wentzel (Eds.), *Social motivation: Understanding children's school adjustment* (pp. 279–312). New York: Cambridge University Press.

Ryan, A. M. (2001). The peer group as a context for the development of young adolescent motivation and achievement. *Child Development, 72,* 1135–1150.

Schmidt, W. H., McKnight, C. C., Cogan, L. S., Jakwerth, P. M., & Houang, R. T. (1999). *Facing the consequences: Using TIMSS for a closer look at U.S. mathematics and science education.* Boston: Kluwer.

HEATHER A. BOUCHEY is assistant professor of psychology at the University of Vermont. Her research focuses on adolescent relationship processes and how they influence individual development and adjustment.

CYNTHIA E. WINSTON is assistant professor of psychology at Howard University and principal investigator of the Identity and Success Research Laboratory. Her research focuses on race self complexity and the psychological significance of race and racism in successful African Americans' internalized narratives of self.

parents messages are unrelated
to child's later engagement in mathematics.

Identity seems to play a larger role,
   academic identity in math
   is a larger role.

Overtime as students get older, their own
interest become more important

parents beliefs are ~~related or~~ do positively
predict interest + competence beliefs in 10th
grade mathematics.

Although these findings point to the already known
belief that parents matter, they leave many
questions

1

Parents' math and science–promotive behaviors predict
children's activities and interest in these courses.

The link between parents beliefs of their
children's abilities and children's self perceptio
has been established by extant literature

Girls' and Boys' Developing Interests in Math and Science: Do Parents Matter?

Janis E. Jacobs, Martha M. Bleeker

Previous studies (for example, Bregman & Killen, 1999; Eccles, Wigfield, & Schiefele, 1998; Jacobs, 1991; Jacobs & Eccles, 2000) have demonstrated the important role that parents' attitudes play in shaping their children's later self-perceptions and achievement behaviors. Studies indicate that in the math and science arena, parents' perceptions of their children's abilities as well as their own values about math and science are related to their children's later self-perceptions and values for achieving in these domains. The previous work suggests that parents are conveying their attitudes and values about math to their children through their words and actions; however, little research has documented the ways in which parents' beliefs and specific behaviors might promote positive achievement attitudes and behaviors in their children. The goal of the study reported here was to document relations between parents' math and science–promotive behaviors and attitudes and their children's later activity choices, values, and achievement in these subjects.

This research was supported by grant HD17553 from the National Institute for Child Health and Human Development to J. S. Eccles, A. Wigfield, P. C. Blumenfeld, and R. D. Harold. The authors would like to thank the principals, teachers, students, and parents of the cooperating school districts for their participation in this project.

The Development of Values and Interest in Math and Science

Numerous theories dealing with competence, expectancy, and control beliefs provide explanations for performance on different kinds of achievement tasks; however, many of these theories do not systematically address another important motivational question: What makes the individual *want* to do the task? Even if people are certain they can do a task, they may not want to engage in it. According to some of the modern expectancy-value theories (for example, Eccles-Parsons et al., 1983; Feather, 1982; Wigfield & Eccles, 1992), an individual's values for particular goals and tasks can help explain *why* a child chooses one activity over another. Wigfield and Eccles (1992) suggest that during the early elementary school grades, the subjective value of a task may be primarily characterized by the child's interest in the task; thus, young children's activity choices may stem from their interests in those activities. When children are young, their interests may shift fairly rapidly, so that children try many different activities for a short time before deciding which activities they enjoy the most. During the early and middle elementary school grades, the child's sense of the usefulness of different activities for future goals may not be very clear; thus this component may only be understood at a later age (Jacobs & Eccles, 2000).

We have found that children value certain tasks less as they get older (see Eccles & Midgley, 1989; Wigfield & Eccles, 1992, for reviews). For example, utility values (usefulness) and attainment values (importance) for math decrease across the elementary school years (Wigfield et al., 1997). We know from our longitudinal analyses that children's beliefs about their own competence and the value they place on mathematics decrease with increasing grade in school (Eccles, Wigfield, Harold, & Blumenfeld, 1993; Jacobs, Lanza, Osgood, Eccles, & Wigfield, 2002), and that gender differences decrease with age. Thus, in the first grade, boys have a more positive view of their math and computer abilities than girls, but by the twelfth grade, many of these differences disappear (Jacobs et al., 2002). Although many achievement beliefs and behaviors could be considered in the current study, the focus is on children's math values; such beliefs have proven to be major predictors of later activity choice and performance, showing that, even after controlling for prior performance levels, task values predict course plans and enrollment decisions in mathematics and physics (Eccles-Parsons et al., 1983; Eccles, Adler, & Meece, 1984; Eccles & Wigfield, 1995; Eccles & Harold, 1991). Thus we have chosen to highlight the role of parent socialization on children's developing interest and values for math and science.

Theoretical and Empirical Background

The Eccles-Parsons et al. model of parent socialization (1983) suggests that the messages parents provide to their children include information regarding the values and importance that the parents attach to activities (for example, math and science). Such messages are likely to be related to a child's motivation to pursue particular activities in the short run. In addition, over time, children are expected to develop their own self-perceptions and interests, based on their parents' messages and behaviors as well as on their own experiences, and these self-perceptions will ultimately affect their future task choices (Jacobs & Eccles, 2000). For example, parents who value math and believe that their children excel at it might convey this to the child by engaging in a range of math-promotive behaviors (for example, positive comments, playing math games with the child, enrolling the child in an engineering camp). Such messages are likely to help children develop high values and more positive self-perceptions of math abilities. Of course, it is important to acknowledge that parents' and children's beliefs are likely to influence each other reciprocally.

According to the Eccles-Parsons model, there are several ways in which parents communicate their beliefs and values about a specific achievement domain to their children: (1) as interpreters of reality; (2) by their provision of particular opportunities; (3) by their involvement in activities with their children; and (4) as role models of valued activities. We have tested and found support for each of the components of parent influence (for example, Eccles-Parsons, Adler, & Kaczala, 1982; Eccles & Jacobs, 1986; Jacobs, 1991; Jacobs & Eccles, 1992). Empirical support for the importance of each of these components is briefly reviewed here.

Interpreters of Reality. One way in which parents influence their children's task values is by acting as "interpreters of reality" through the messages they provide regarding their perceptions of their children's world and experiences (Eccles, Lord, Roeser, Barber, & Jozefowicz, 1997; Goodnow & Collins, 1990; Phillips, 1987). When children are young, they are not particularly good at assessing their own competence (Nicholls, 1978), so they must rely on their parents' interpretations of their performance as a major source of information about their competence. In addition, parents' beliefs about the world may color their views of their children's abilities, and the ways they think children should spend their time.

For example, Jacobs (1991) explored the relation between parents' gender stereotypes and parents' and children's ability perceptions of math and found that parents who held traditional gender stereotypes favoring males in mathematics expressed less confidence in their children's math abilities if they had daughters and more confidence if they had sons, regardless of their children's actual abilities and performance levels. In a recent study, Bleeker and Jacobs (2004) followed the same families over an extended period and found that after controlling for parents' gender stereotypes, parents' earlier perceptions of their children's abilities were related to their daughters' career choices twelve years later.

We have found that in addition to the role played by parents' general beliefs about the world, parents' perceptions of their own children's math abilities and their expectations for their children's future successes in math have a large impact on children's developing perceptions of self-competence (for example, Eccles-Parsons et al., 1982; Jacobs & Eccles, 1992). In these studies, parents' perceptions of their children's abilities, their expectations for their children's success, and their gender stereotypes predicted children's self-perceptions of competence and their actual math achievement, even after previous indicators of achievement were controlled. Although parents are clearly forming their opinions about the child's ability based on objective indicators such as grades, it appears that the direction of influence for perceptions of competence is from parents to children and that parents' views of their children's abilities are quite stable over time (Yoon, Wigfield, & Eccles, 1993).

Provision of Opportunities. Parents structure children's experiences in a variety of ways that should have an impact on self and task values, interests, and skill acquisition. Although it seems obvious that children need to be exposed to an activity if they are to become interested in it, the way in which such exposure affects preferences and activity choices is not clear. Exposure may occur when parents provide opportunities for their children by purchasing toys and games. For example, parents who value math may purchase computer games, board games, or other manipulative materials that involve math. Earlier research (for example, Bradley & Caldwell, 1984) suggests that such strategies can have an effect on later achievement if employed early in life, and they are likely to have similar effects at later ages.

The type of toys, activities, and opportunities parents provide will depend on many factors: what is available in the community, economic resources (many activities and equipment for activities have high costs), time constraints (single parents, two-earner families, and families with many children have less time to devote to any given activity), parents' values for a particular endeavor, and gender of the child and parent. For example, parents often provide experiences for their children that fit existing expectations for gender-appropriate toys (for example, dolls for girls, computer games for boys) and activities (dance classes for girls, Peewee football for boys) (see Eccles, 1993; Jacobs, Vernon, & Eccles, in press; Jodl, Michael, Malanchuk, Eccles, & Sameroff, 2001). These gender-differentiated experiences give boys and girls the opportunity to practice different skills, thus affecting their knowledge, expectations, preferences, and abilities (Leaper, 2002; Serbin, Zelkowitz, Doyle, & Gold, 1990).

Parents' perceptions of their children's abilities and interests also are likely to affect the types of experiences parents provide. In one study, parents were more likely to provide extra sports experiences for their children if they believed that the children were interested in the activity and had sports ability (Fredericks, 1999). This is a good example of the reciprocal nature of parent-child attitudes: parents are using the feedback they receive from the child, as well as their own assessment of the child, to inform their decisions about which opportunities to provide.

Parental Involvement in Children's Activities. Yet another way in which parents communicate their beliefs about the importance of particular activities and their perceptions of the child's abilities is by choosing to participate in activities *with* their children (Ginsburg & Bronstein, 1993; Okagaki & Sternberg, 1993). Recent literature indicates that parental involvement may influence children's leisure activities and achievement behaviors. For instance, Larson, Dworkin, and Gillman (2001) found that the amount of time single mothers spend in child-supportive activities was positively associated with adolescents' constructive use of free time. Evidence also indicates that greater parental involvement in children's learning positively affects children's school performance, including both greater cognitive performance and higher academic achievement (Eccles & Harold, 1996; Griffith, 1996; Moles, 1996). For example, children learn science more quickly and confidently when they do science-based activities with their parents at home (Dierking & Falk, 1994). Crowley, Callanan, Tenenbaum, and Allen (2001) reported that parents who involved children in science activities not only provided opportunities for children to learn about science but also helped children develop scientific interests and values. Finally, using retrospective reports from young adults, Ferry, Fouad, and Smith (2000) found that parental encouragement in math and science influenced offspring's learning experiences, which in turn influenced self-efficacy and outcome expectations.

Gender differences related to parental involvement have been reported, but the results are mixed, sometimes suggesting that fathers are generally less involved and spend less time in play activities with children than mothers (Kazura, 2000). However, some researchers (for example, Fagot, Rodgers, & Leinbach, 2000) have found that fathers spend a significant amount of playtime with children and may be more important to children's gender-role development than mothers, despite the fact that mothers spend more time in general with children. Other researchers (for example, McHale, Crouter, & Whiteman, 2003) believe that gender differences within families are best understood in terms of the transactional patterns of the family as a whole.

Although such parental participation at home is generally viewed as important (Epstein, 1990), only the parental activities that are interpreted by children as supportive are positively correlated with children's actual performance (Campbell & Mandel, 1990). For example, unsolicited homework help given to children may be interpreted as an indication that the child actually needs help, and may have negative effects on children's self-perceptions (Graham, 1990). Indeed, Epstein (1988) found a negative relationship between student achievement in math and reading and parental help with homework. Similarly, Desimone (1999) found that having parents who checked homework regularly was negatively related to achievement, regardless of the family's ethnicity or income level. These findings highlight the bidirectional nature of parent-child influences. When parents see that their children are not trying hard enough or are failing despite high effort, parents may intensify their involvement or change tactics.

Modeling Involvement in Valued Activities. Finally, the importance of role models in socializing behavior has been well documented in the developmental literature (for example, Bandura & Walters, 1963). This involves the parents participating in the activities for their own sake and on their own, rather than to help their children. According to this perspective, parents exhibit behaviors that children may later imitate and adopt as part of their own repertoire. The ways in which parents spend their time, the choices they make between available activities, and the sense of self-competence that they project send strong messages to their children about activities that are valued and about acceptable ways to spend time. For example, children who see their parents carry out household math activities (such as balancing a checkbook) believe that their parents like math more than those whose parents do not engage in math activities at home (Eccles-Parsons et al., 1982).

Current Study

Although previous research indicates that parents' beliefs and behaviors have a powerful impact on their children's interests, values, and activity choices, less is known about the ways parents communicate these perceptions to their children. Research in domains other than math and science (for example, sports and physical activity) suggests that parents' involvement with their children, their modeling activities, and the items parents purchase for children should be associated with children's later math and science interests, values, and activities. Thus the current study examined the relations between parents' attitudes, activity involvement, purchases, and children's later math and science interests and activities. We also examined gender differences within the family, based on the literature reviewed earlier suggesting that mothers' and fathers' involvement may have differential effects on their sons' and daughters' beliefs. The following research questions formed the basis of our inquiry: (1) Do the math and science toys mothers purchase for their children differ by child's sex and grade in school? (2) Do the activities in which parents participate with their children vary by child's sex, child's grade, and parents' sex? (3) Are parental involvement, parental modeling, and opportunities provided by parents related to children's later interests and involvement in math and science activities?

Method

These data were collected as part of the Childhood and Beyond (CAB) study, a longitudinal investigation of the development of children's self-perceptions, task values, and activity choices (Eccles-Parsons et al., 1983).

Participants. Beginning in 1983, children, parents, and teachers were recruited through ten elementary schools in the greater Detroit area. A cross-sequential design was employed, in which three cohorts of children were followed longitudinally across the elementary, middle, and high school years. All children in kindergarten, grade one, and grade three were asked to participate, and 75 percent of the children both agreed to participate and obtained parental permission. The original sample consisted of 53 percent girls and 47 percent boys, and these proportions remained the same throughout the waves of data collection. Information about income provided by the school districts indicates that the children were from middle-class backgrounds with average family income of $50,000 at the initial time of data collection. Over 95 percent of the children were European American. Attrition in the sample was due mostly to children's moving far away from the school districts sampled, although every effort was made to relocate children each year. The longitudinal sample included children who continued to live in the same general area, even if they no longer attended participating schools.

Procedure. Each spring, children and parents completed questionnaires measuring their competence beliefs, values, and interest in math. The analyses reported here are based on items drawn from the surveys given during Years 2, 4, and 8 of the study. Children completed the questionnaires in their classrooms in the participating schools. All items were answered using 7-point response scales that had been developed by Eccles and her colleagues in earlier studies to assess children's and adolescents' beliefs. The original items had good psychometric properties (see Eccles et al., 1984; Eccles-Parsons et al., 1983; Eccles & Wigfield, 1995; Eccles et al., 1993; Eccles-Parsons et al., 1982). Questions were read aloud to the youngest cohort in Year 2; all other children read the questions on their own. The questionnaires were administered in three sessions during the school day, lasting twenty minutes each. In addition, each year of the study parents received surveys in the mail to complete and return.

Measures

The analyses reported here are based on items drawn from the surveys parents completed during Year 2 that specifically assessed parents' values, beliefs about their children, purchases, and activities in math and science; parents' reports of their children's math and science involvement during Year 4 of the study; and children's reported perceptions of their math interest during Years 2 and 8 of the study.

Items Purchased. During Year 2, parents were asked to indicate if they had purchased particular types of math and science items (for example, science books, math games) for their child in the past year. The number of items checked created a variable ranging from 0 to 4.

Parents' Math and Science Activities with Children. During Year 2, parents were asked to answer one question about how often they participated in math and science activities with their children, ranging from 1 = Never, to 6 = Almost every day.

Parents' Math Modeling. During Year 2, mothers and fathers were asked to report how often they participated in math and science activities themselves (at home), ranging from never to 20+ hours. This item was recoded for use in the later analyses; recoding procedures are described in detail in the results section.

Parents' Perceptions of Child's Math Ability. This scale, measuring parents' perceptions of their children's abilities in mathematics during Year 2, was created and validated in Eccles's earlier studies. The scale consists of four items (for example, "How good is your child in math?"), each answered with a 7-point Likert Scale (1 = Not at all good, 7 = Very good). Cronbach's alphas for mothers and fathers on this scale were .93 and .92, respectively, indicating high construct validity.

Parents' Math Value. Parents' math value was measured at Year 2 with a single item that asked parents how important it was for their child to do well in math. This item was answered with a 7-point Likert Scale.

Children's Math and Science Activities. This measure, given during Year 4 of the study, included four items that asked parents to report how often their child was involved in math and science activities (for example, math and science pleasure activities) outside of school each week. The responses for these four items, which each ranged from 0 to 25 hours a week, were added together to obtain a total amount of time children were involved in math and science activities during an average week.

Children's Math Interest. Two versions of this measure, previously used by Eccles, were used to measure children's mathematics interest during Year 2 and Year 8. At Year 2, two items (for example, "How much do you like math?") were answered on a 7-point Likert Scale (1 = A little, 7 = A lot). At Year 8, this scale consisted of four questions, similar to those in Year 2. Cronbach's alphas for these scales at Year 2 and Year 8 were .73 and .89, respectively, indicating good construct validity.

Results

Do the math and science toys mothers purchase for their children differ by child's sex and grade in school?

Due to the fact that parents purchase only one set of math and science toys for their children, only one parent reporter was used for this variable (although each parent responded to the question individually). We chose to use mothers' reports because more mothers than fathers participated in the study and because mothers are more likely to purchase toys or be aware of toys purchased. Univariate analyses of variance (ANOVAs) were performed with grade level and child's sex as the between-subjects independent variables, and mothers' math and science purchases as the dependent variable. As can be seen in Figure 1.1, mothers were more likely to purchase math and science items for sons than for daughters, regardless of the child's grade in school [$F(1, 557) = 13.57$, $p < .001$]. Although mothers' purchasing

Figure 1.1. Mothers' Math and Science Purchases for Child by Grade and Gender

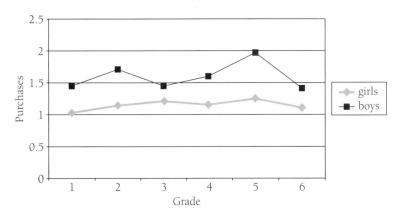

patterns fluctuated throughout the time period between first and sixth grades, there was no significant main effect of grade. In addition, no significant interaction between child's sex and grade in school was found.

Do the activities in which parents participate with their children vary by child's sex, child's grade, and parents' sex?

Repeated measures ANOVAs were used to examine relationships between mothers' and fathers' involvement with their children, using grade level and child's sex as between-subjects independent variables, parent's sex as a within-subjects variable, and activity involvement as the dependent variable. As seen in Figure 1.2, significant grade differences existed for both mothers and fathers, indicating that parents' involvement in math and science activities varied by child's grade in school. Tukey post-hoc tests indicate that both mothers and fathers were more likely to indicate involvement in children's math and science activities during the third and fourth grades than during the sixth grade [F(1, 247) = 15.75, $p < .001$]. In addition, mothers and fathers were more likely to be involved in daughters' math and science activities than sons' activities [F(1, 247) = 3.67, $p < .05$]. There were no significant differences between mothers' and fathers' math and science activities with their children.

Are parental involvement, parental modeling, and opportunities provided by parents related to children's later interests and involvement in math and science activities?

To examine the association between parents' promotive activities (that is, math and science involvement, purchases, and modeling) and children's math and science activities two years later, hierarchical regression analyses were conducted separately for mothers and fathers.

The first set of regressions examined the association between parents' purchases, involvement, and modeling, and parents' reports of their children's

Figure 1.2. (a) Mothers' Math and Science Activities with Children (b) Fathers' Math and Science Activities with Children

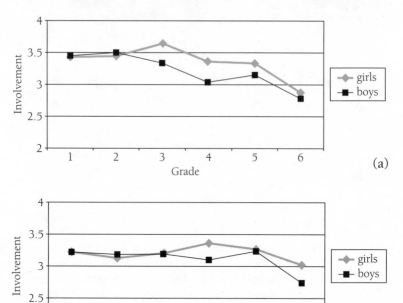

(a)

(b)

involvement in math and science activities two years later. For this analysis, parents' purchases and involvement were recoded and combined into one variable, because of the significant positive correlation between these two variables. The items purchased were recoded so that the variable ranged from 0 to 2 (0 = No items, 1 = One item, and 2 = Two, three, or four items purchased). The involvement variable was also recoded so that it ranged from 0 to 2 (0 = Never, 1 = Occasionally/2–3 times a month, and 2 = Weekly or daily). After these two variables had been recoded, they were added together to create the math and science purchases and activities variable that is used in the regression analyses (range = 0–4).

Our goal was to examine the potential contributions made by parents' attitudes and behaviors; thus we chose to control for major preexisting factors (that is, sex of child [1 = female, 2 = male], grade in school, and prior math interest) that we knew would be related to the child's current math interest. Specifically, block one contained child's sex and grade, block two contained child's math interest at Year 2, block three contained parent's math value and parent's perceptions of child's math ability at Year 2, and block four contained parent's math modeling behaviors and parent's purchases and activities at Year 2. As can be seen in Table 1.1, both mothers'

Table 1.1 Role of Parent Beliefs and Behaviors on Children's Activities and Interests

	Children's Activities (Y4)		Children's Math Interests (Y8)	
	Mom	Dad	Mom	Dad
Block 1				
Child's sex	.07	.10	−.12*	−.14*
Cohort	.05	.10	−.13*	−.09
Block 2				
Child's math interest (Y2)	.07	.09	.32***	.29***
Block 3				
Parent's math value (Y2)	.01	.06	−.04	−.06
Parent's perception of child's math ability (Y2)	−.04	.04	.08	.04
Block 4				
Parent's time in math modeling (Y2)	.17**	.13	−.06	.08
Parent's math and science purchases and activities (Y2)	.21***	.19**	.13*	.02
R-square	.10	.09	.16	.12

*p < .5; **p < .01; ***p < .001

math modeling and purchases and activities at Year 2 were significant predictors of children's math involvement at Year 4. Similarly, the variable measuring math purchases and activities was a significant predictor in the fathers' model. The positive coefficients indicate that being around mothers who engage in math activities, engaging in math activities with both parents, and owning math and science toys are associated with greater math and science involvement two years later.

The next set of regressions examined the association between parents' purchases, involvement, and modeling and children's reported interests in math six years later (Year 8), following the transition to middle school. The regression model and predictor variables were identical to those used in the prior analyses, and regressions were once again conducted separately for mothers and fathers. As can be seen in Table 1.1, child's sex, grade, and math interest six years earlier were significant predictors of math interest at Year 8. The negative beta weights for sex and grade indicate that girls and children in earlier grades report more math interests than boys and children in later grades. The significant, positive coefficient for math and science purchases and activities in the model for mothers indicates that children's math interests increase as mothers purchase math and science toys and become involved in their children's math and science activities.

Neither fathers' activities with children nor mothers' and fathers' modeling were significant predictors of children's interests in math six years later. It should also be noted that these models account for only small proportions of the variance in children's participation in math and science activities.

Discussion

We began this chapter by asking the question that appears in the title: Do parents matter? Although earlier studies have pointed to the importance of parents' perceptions and beliefs for their children's later math and science achievement, little empirical evidence has been available regarding the ways in which parents convey these attitudes to their children through specific behaviors, or to tell us if specific parenting behaviors are related to later involvement or interests in math and science activities. The goal of this study was to document relations between parents' math and science–promotive behaviors and attitudes and their children's later interests and activity choices related to these subjects.

The short answer to the overarching question is a resounding "Yes, parents matter": their specific math-promotive behaviors are related to their children's later interests and activities. Of course, the longer answer has many more qualifications and nuances, creating a rather complicated but more interesting picture. The more complex version of the answer must include two important trends that we discuss in greater detail in this section: (1) parents' promotive activities depend on the gender of their child and the gender of the parent, and (2) parents' promotive behaviors are related to their children's later interests and involvement in math and science activities.

The results of this study make it clear that *parents' promotive activities depend on the gender of their child and the gender of the parent.* We found that parents (as reported by mothers) were more likely to purchase math and science items for sons than for daughters, regardless of the child's grade in school. These findings suggest that boys in this study may have had greater opportunities than girls to practice math skills, which, according to some researchers (Leaper, 2002; Serbin et al., 1990), lead children to have different knowledge, expectations, preferences, and abilities in this arena. The gender-differentiated provision of math-related toys and activities is especially surprising in light of the fact that our regression analyses revealed that girls are significantly more interested in math and science than are boys.

Although boys were provided with more opportunities to experience math and science toys, the reverse was true for parental involvement in math and science activities with their children. On average, both mothers and fathers were more likely to be involved in daughters' math and science activities than in sons' activities. This may have been due to parents' perceptions that daughters needed more help in this area. This interpretation would support others' findings (for example, Desimone, 1999; Epstein, 1988; Hoover-Dempsey & Sandler, 1995) that parents are more likely to become involved in activities with their children if they believe that their children need help, and that unsolicited homework help given to children may be interpreted as an indication that the child actually needs help, and may have negative effects on children's self-perceptions (Graham, 1990). It should also be noted that involvement in such activities did not differ by the parent's gender; mothers and fathers were equally likely to be involved. This supports the findings of some researchers (for example, Fagot et al., 2000) who have reported few gender differences in parental involvement with children.

A second major theme that is apparent in our findings is that *parents' promotive behaviors are related to their children's later interests and involvement in math and science activities.* Although such behaviors did not explain large amounts of the variance in children's interests and involvement, some of the behaviors contributed to the equations even after controlling for the child's gender, earlier interest in math and science, and parents' beliefs. Interestingly, the purchases and activities provided by the parents were the most consistent predictors of involvement in math two years later and of interest in math six years later (mothers' model only). The amount of time mothers spent modeling math behaviors also predicted their children's involvement in math two years later. These findings are consistent with our earlier research (for example, Eccles-Parsons et al., 1982; Eccles et al., 1997; Eccles & Jacobs, 1986; Jacobs, 1991; Jacobs & Eccles, 1992) showing that parents' attitudes are related to their children's later achievement beliefs and behaviors. The current findings also extend the earlier work by moving beyond parental attitudes to include the specific promotive behaviors in which parents are involved. Therefore, both attitudes and actions seem to play a role in shaping children's achievement choices.

In summary, we found support for the idea that parents' math and science–promotive behaviors are related to their children's later interests and involvement in these activities. In addition, these data make it clear that the opportunities parents provided, parental modeling, and parental involvement in activities depend on the gender of the child and the gender of the parent. Although gender differences in achievement and interest in mathematics and science have diminished over the past decade (see Jacobs et al., 2002), it appears that parental practices in these arenas remain "gendered," leading us to conclude that although parents matter, the specifics about what is provided and what matters may differ for girls and boys.

New Directions

Although these findings point to the importance of studying parents' attitudes and beliefs, as well as their math-promotive activities, they leave many questions unanswered and suggest new directions for future research. For example, any of the relations reported here could be due to the fact that parents engage in promotive behaviors primarily as a reaction to their children's interest. Although in the regression analyses we controlled for earlier interests on the part of the children and for parents' perceptions of their children's abilities, we do not have earlier measures of parental promotive behaviors to see if these changed in response to the child. As we have suggested elsewhere (for example, Jacobs & Eccles, 2000), it is likely that parents' promotive activities and children's interests and achievement are reciprocal and interactive. Future research should investigate the reciprocal effects of parents' and children's activities and beliefs over time. In addition, studies that include parents' perceptions of whether they are "leading" or "following" their children's interests would be helpful. If parents believe that they are only responding to their children's interests and abilities, it may be important to help them understand the important role they play in shaping such interests.

Another direction for further research in this area is to examine the ways in which different combinations of math-promotive behaviors (such as help with homework, modeling, attitudes) done by mothers versus fathers may result in different outcomes for daughters or sons. Bandura's model and studies (Bandura & Walters, 1963) indicate that the gender of the parent, the specific activity, and the relationship with the child will affect the impact of role modeling. The same differences are likely to be found for parents' math-promotive behaviors. It would also be helpful to see if the same patterns of relationships between parent-child beliefs and activities hold in families from different socioeconomic backgrounds. The families in the study reported here were primarily middle to upper-middle class; thus they may communicate their values to their children by spending free time on particular activities or by purchasing certain items. In families with limited financial means, these avenues for sharing values may not be available. It is important to test these ideas in a more diverse sample or in one with more limited economic resources. In such a sample, attitudes rather than actions may play a larger role.

As is true of most research, we can conclude that we answered the original question (yes, parents matter), but we are left with many more interesting questions for future studies: Exactly what matters and under what conditions? When will math-promotive behaviors backfire, and when will they produce long-term interest in the topic? Who will benefit from specific behaviors or attitudes? How important is the gender of the parent or child? This study reminds us that when it comes to those more difficult questions about parents' roles in their children's developing math and science interests, we have much to learn.

References

Bandura, A., & Walters, R. H. (1963). *Social learning and personality development.* Austin, Tex.: Holt, Rinehart and Winston.

Bleeker, M. M. & Jacobs, J. E. (2004). Achievement in math and science: Do mothers' beliefs matter twelve years later? *Journal of Educational Psychology, 96(1),* 97–109.

Bradley, R. H., & Caldwell, B. M. (1984). The relation of infants' home environment to achievement test performance in first grade: A follow-up study. *Child Development, 55,* 803–809.

Bregman, G., & Killen, M. (1999). Adolescents' and young adults' reasoning about career choice and the role of parental influence. *Journal of Research on Adolescence, 9,* 253–275.

Campbell, J., & Mandel, F. (1990). Connecting math achievement to parental influences. *Contemporary Educational Psychology, 15,* 64–74.

Crowley, K., Callanan, M. A., Tenenbaum, H. R., & Allen, E. (2001). Parents explain more often to boys than to girls during shared scientific thinking. *Psychological Science, 12,* 258–261.

Desimone, L. (1999). Linking parental involvement with student academic achievement: Do race and income matter? *Journal of Educational Research, 93,* 11–30.

Dierking, L. D., & Falk, J. H. (1994). Family behavior and learning in informal science settings: A review of the research. *Science Education, 78,* 57–76.

Eccles, J. S. (1993). School and family effects on the ontogeny of children's interests, self-perceptions, and activity choices. In R. Dienstbier & J. E. Jacobs (Eds.), *Developmental perspectives on motivation* (Vol. 40, pp. 145–208). Lincoln: University of Nebraska Press.

Eccles, J. S., Adler, T. F., & Meece, J. L. (1984). Sex differences in achievement: A test of alternative theories. *Journal of Personality and Social Psychology, 46,* 26–43.

Eccles, J. S., & Harold, R. D. (1991). Gender differences in sport involvement: Applying the Eccles expectancy-value model. *Journal of Applied Sport Psychology, 3,* 7–35.

Eccles, J. S., & Harold, R. D. (1996). Family involvement in children's and adolescents' schooling. In A. Booth & J. F. Dunn (Eds.), *Family-school links: How do they affect educational outcomes?* (pp. 3–34). Mahwah, NJ: Erlbaum.

Eccles, J. S., & Jacobs, J. E. (1986). Social forces shape math attitudes and performance. *Signs: Journal of Women in Culture and Society, 11,* 367–380.

Eccles, J. S., Lord, S. E., Roeser, R. W., Barber, B. L., & Jozefowicz, D. M. (1997). The association of school transitions in early adolescence with developmental trajectories through high school. In J. Schulenberg, J. L. Maggs, & K. Hurrelmann (Eds.), *Health risks and developmental transitions during adolescence* (pp. 283–321). New York: Cambridge University Press.

Eccles, J. S., & Midgley, C. (1989). Stage/environment fit: Developmentally appropriate classrooms for early adolescents. In R. Ames & C. Ames (Eds.), *Research on motivation in education* (Vol. 3, pp. 139–181). Orlando: Academic Press.

Eccles, J. S., & Wigfield, A. (1995). In the mind of the achiever: The structure of adolescents' academic achievement-related beliefs and self-perceptions. *Personality and Social Psychology Bulletin, 21,* 215–225.

Eccles, J. S., Wigfield, A., Harold, R. D., & Blumenfeld, P. C. (1993). Age and gender differences in children's achievement self-perceptions during the elementary school years. *Child Development, 64,* 830–847.

Eccles, J. S., Wigfield, A., & Schiefele, U. (1998). Motivation to succeed. In W. Damon (Series Ed.) & N. Eisenberg (Vol. Ed.), *Handbook of child psychology:* Vol. 3. *Social, emotional, and personality development* (5th ed., pp. 1017–1095). New York: Wiley.

Eccles-Parsons, J., Adler, T. F., Futterman, R., Goff, S. B., Kaczala, C. M., Meece, J. L., & Midgley, C. (1983). Expectancies, values, and academic behaviors. In J. T. Spence (Ed.), *Achievement and achievement motives: Psychological and sociological approaches* (pp. 75–146). San Francisco: Freeman.

Eccles-Parsons, J., Adler, T. F., & Kaczala, C. M. (1982). Socialization of achievement attitudes and beliefs: Parental influences. *Child Development, 53,* 322–339.

Epstein, J. L. (1988). *Homework practices, achievements, and behavior of elementary school students* (Report No. 26). Baltimore: Center for Research on Elementary and Middle Schools, Johns Hopkins University.

Epstein, J. L. (1990). School and family connections: Theory, research, and implications for integrating sociologies of education and family. In D. G. Unger & M. B. Sussman (Eds.), *Families in community settings: Interdisciplinary perspectives* (pp. 99–126). Binghamton, NY: Haworth Press.

Fagot, B. I., Rodgers, C. S., & Leinbach, M. D. (2000). Theories of gender socialization. In T. Eckes & H. M. Trautner (Eds.), *The developmental social psychology of gender* (pp. 65–89). Mahwah, NJ: Erlbaum.

Feather, N. T. (1982). Expectancy-value approaches: Present status and future directions. In N. T. Feather (Ed.), *Expectations and actions: Expectancy-value models in psychology* (pp. 395–420). Mahwah, NJ: Erlbaum.

Ferry, T. R., Fouad, N. A., & Smith, P. L. (2000). The role of family context in a social cognitive model for a career-related choice behavior: A math and science perspective. *Journal of Vocational Behavior, 57*, 348–364.

Fredericks, J. (1999). *"Girl-friendly" family contexts: Socialization into math and sports.* Unpublished doctoral dissertation, University of Michigan, Ann Arbor.

Ginsburg, G., & Bronstein, P. (1993). Family factors related to children's intrinsic/extrinsic motivational orientation and academic performance. *Child Development, 64*, 1461–1474.

Goodnow, J. J., & Collins, W. A. (1990). Development according to parents: The nature, sources, and consequences of parents' ideas. London: Erlbaum.

Graham, S. (1990). Communicating low ability in the classroom: Bad things good teachers sometimes do. In S. Graham & V. Folkes (Eds.), *Attribution theory: Applications to achievement, mental health, and interpersonal conflict* (pp. 17–36). Mahwah, NJ: Erlbaum.

Griffith, J. (1996). Relation of parental involvement, empowerment, and school traits to student academic performance. *Journal of Educational Research, 90*, 33–41.

Hoover-Dempsey, K. V., & Sandler, H. M. (1995). Parental involvement in children's education: Why does it make a difference? *Teachers College Record, 97*, 310–331.

Jacobs, J. E. (1991). The influence of gender stereotypes on parent and child math attitudes: Differences across grade-levels. *Journal of Educational Psychology, 83*, 518–527.

Jacobs, J. E., & Eccles, J. S. (1992). The influence of parent stereotypes on parent and child ability beliefs in three domains. *Journal of Personality and Social Psychology, 63*, 932–944.

Jacobs, J. E., & Eccles, J. S. (2000). Parents, task values, and real-life achievement-related choices. In C. Sansone & J. M. Harackiewicz (Eds.), *Intrinsic and extrinsic motivation: The search for optimal motivation and performance* (pp. 405–439). Orlando: Academic Press.

Jacobs, J. E., Lanza, S., Osgood, D. W., Eccles, J. S., & Wigfield, A. (2002). Changes in children's self-competence and values: Gender and domain differences across grades one through twelve. *Child Development, 73*, 509–527.

Jacobs, J. E., Vernon, M. K., & Eccles, J. S. (in press). Gender differences in activity involvement during middle childhood: Longitudinal links between time spent, mothers' beliefs, self-beliefs, and activity preferences. In J. L. Mahoney, J. S. Eccles, and R. Larson (Eds.), *After-school activities: Contexts of development.* Mahwah, NJ: Erlbaum.

Jodl, K. M., Michael, A., Malanchuk, O., Eccles, J. S., & Sameroff, A. (2001). Parents' roles in shaping early adolescents' occupational aspirations. *Child Development, 72*, 1247–1265.

Kazura, K. (2000). Fathers' qualitative and quantitative involvement: An investigation of attachment, play, and social interactions. *Journal of Men's Studies, 9*, 41–57.

Larson, R., Dworkin, J., & Gillman, S. (2001). Facilitating adolescents' constructive use of time in one-parent families. *Applied Developmental Science, 5*(3), 143–157.

Leaper, C. (2002). Parenting girls and boys. In M. H. Bornstein (Ed.), *Handbook of parenting: Vol. 1. Children and parenting* (pp. 189–225). Mahwah, NJ: Erlbaum.

McHale, S. M., Crouter, A. C., & Whiteman, S. D. (2003). The family contexts of gender development in childhood and adolescence. *Social Development, 12*(1), 125–148.

Moles, O. C. (1996). New national directions in research and policy. In A. Booth & J. F. Dunn (Eds.), *Family-school links: How do they affect educational outcomes?* (pp. 247–254). Mahwah, NJ: Erlbaum.

Nicholls, J. G. (1978). The development of the concepts of effort and ability, perceptions of academic attainment, and the understanding that difficult tasks require more ability. *Child Development, 49*, 800–814.

Okagaki, L., & Sternberg, R. (1993). Parental beliefs and children's school performance. *Child Development, 64*, 36–56.

Phillips, D. A. (1987). Socialization of perceived academic competence among highly competent children. *Child Development, 58*, 1308–1320.

Serbin, L. A., Zelkowitz, P., Doyle, A. B., & Gold, D. (1990). The socialization of sex-differentiated skills and academic performance: A mediational model. *Sex Roles, 23*, 613–628.

Wigfield, A., & Eccles, J. S. (1992). The development of achievement task values: A theoretical analysis. *Developmental Review, 12*, 265–310.

Wigfield, A., Eccles, J. S., Yoon, K. S., Harold, R. D., Arbreton, A. J., Freedman-Doan, C., & Blumenfeld, P. C. (1997). Change in children's competence beliefs and subjective task values across the elementary school years: A three-year study. *Journal of Educational Psychology, 89*, 451–469.

Yoon, K. S., Wigfield, A., & Eccles, J. S. (1993, April). *Causal relations between mothers' and children's beliefs about math ability: A structural equation model.* Paper presented at the annual meeting of the American Educational Research Association, Atlanta, GA.

JANIS E. JACOBS *is professor of human development and family studies, professor of psychology, and vice provost for undergraduate education and international programs at Pennsylvania State University.*

MARTHA M. BLEEKER *is a doctoral candidate in human development and family studies at Pennsylvania State University.*

2

The peer context plays an important role in adolescents' views of math and social domains.

Gender Intensification of Peer Socialization During Puberty

Lisa M. Pettitt

Gender differences are a provocative subject with good reason: they are implicated as contributors to important societal problems. Gender differences in math achievement contribute to limited career options for women (Center for Early Adolescence, 1984; Stipp, 1992), which may in turn affect their economic self-sufficiency. Gender differences in social norms about competition and closeness contribute to power and communication problems in female-male relationships, with consequences for family stability and domestic violence (Leaper, 1994). Understanding the origins of gender differences, therefore, has important societal implications.

The Gender Intensification Hypothesis and Puberty

Gender differences in math (achievement domain) and in intimacy and self-disclosure (social domain) tend to emerge or grow during adolescence after the age of twelve, with more significant differences appearing in high school (Eccles, 1989; Hill & Lynch, 1983; Hyde, Fennema, & Lamon, 1990; Hyde, Fennema, Ryan, Frost, & Hopp, 1990). Relatedly, puberty is a hallmark of adolescence, typically beginning between the ages of eight and sixteen and ending between the ages of eighteen and twenty-two. Girls, as compared to boys, typically start puberty one to two years earlier and have growth spurts that occur at an earlier stage and last longer (Fechner, 2002).

Given the co-occurrence of emerging gender differences and pubertal maturation during adolescence, it is not surprising that developmental psychologists have considered the possibility that they are linked. Hill and Lynch's gender intensification hypothesis (1983) posits that the physical

New Directions for Child and Adolescent Development, no. 106, Winter 2004 © Wiley Periodicals, Inc.   23 changes of puberty are viewed as a signal that the adolescent is transitioning into adulthood and adult gender roles (Hill & Lynch, 1983; Galambos, Almeida, & Petersen, 1990). In turn, gender-appropriate role expectations on the part of significant others become stronger and contribute to gender differences in achievement and social domains. The implications of puberty for gender socialization will vary depending on individuals' perceptions of pubertal changes and their perceptions of socialization agents' expectations (Alsaker, 1996).

Hill and Lynch (1983) noted a dearth of studies attempting empirically to link puberty to changes in gender-role expectations. Two decades later, there continue to be few studies of changes in gender socialization during puberty (see Lytton & Romney, 1991, for an exception), and those that do exist have focused primarily on the role of parents. Although it is well documented that peers play a growing and key role in the lives of adolescents (Brown, 1990; Hill & Lynch, 1983), no studies have examined whether adolescents experience an intensification of gender socialization from peers during puberty.

Current Study

The current study tested the gender intensification hypothesis by examining the relationship between adolescents' pubertal status and their perceptions of peer messages about math and social domains. Adolescents' perceptions of peer messages were assessed instead of reports from peers themselves, in accordance with Hill and Lynch's argument (1983) that perceived messages can be more meaningful than actual messages.

Perceived peer messages about the individual adolescent as well as about what is appropriate for girls and boys generally were assessed; research indicates that both types of messages influence self-perceptions (Jacobs & Eccles, 1992; Pettitt, 2001). Three types of peer messages about individual adolescents were measured: (1) the domain's importance to the adolescent, (2) perceptions of the adolescent's ability in the domain, and (3) expectations for the adolescent's career. They were selected because they are associated with the domain's value to the adolescent, which in turn is associated with her or his achievement-related choices (Eccles-Parsons et al., 1983; Eccles, 1989).

Female and male peer messages were measured separately because some evidence suggests that they may be different. Males are more likely than females to stereotype math as a male domain, particularly during adolescence (Hyde, Fennema, Ryan, et al., 1990), and females convey stronger expectations about intimacy than do males (Blyth & Traeger, 1988).

Math and social domains were chosen due to their association with central aspects of masculine and feminine gender-role stereotypes, respectively (Matlin, 1993), and because gender differences in these domains emerge during adolescence, when boys tend to outperform girls in advanced mathematics, and girls' relationships, as compared to boys', become characterized by greater intimacy and self-disclosure.

The hypotheses guiding this study were as follows: (1) with pubertal maturation, boys will report that positive peer messages about the math domain increase, whereas girls will report that messages remain stable or decline; (2) with pubertal maturation, girls will report that positive peer messages about the social domain increase, whereas boys will report that messages remain stable or decline. Given these hypothesized gender differences in peer messages, it is expected that by the end of puberty, boys will report more positive math messages and girls will report more positive social messages, as compared to the other gender. No hypotheses were made about differences in adolescents' perceptions of female and male peers' messages, given the lack of extant research on gender intensification of peer socialization. However, differences were examined.

Method

The current study was a cross-sectional, single-assessment design. There were 335 participants. The participants were students from a public school district in a suburban metropolitan area in the West (85 fourth and fifth graders, 101 sixth through eighth graders, and 149 tenth through twelfth graders). Participating schools fed into one another. The vast majority of the students identified as Caucasian (91 percent); 56 percent were female; 79 percent indicated that their parents were married; 62 percent indicated that their mother had either a college or advanced degree.

Measures. Sample sizes, means, and standard deviations for all variables are listed by participant gender in Table 2.1.

Pubertal Development. Pubertal development was assessed using a modified version of the Pubertal Development Scale (Petersen, Crockett, Richards, & Boxer, 1988). The self-report measure consisted of five items, three of which were the same for girls and boys (growth in height, pubic hair, and skin changes). Girls were also asked about breast development and menarche, and boys were also asked about facial hair growth and voice change. Due to concerns of elementary school staff, elementary students were asked only about growth in height, skin changes, and "other changes in your body." There were four response options: 1 = no development thus far; 2 = development barely begun; 3 = development definitely under way; and 4 = development already complete. For menarche, item response options consisted only of "no development thus far" and "development definitely under way." Higher scores indicated more complete development. In the study sample, internal consistency alphas were .85 for middle and high school students and .67 for elementary school students. Pubertal status was significantly correlated with age (r = .76 for girls; r = .71 for boys).

The pubertal items were also used to generate a categorical score representing one of five stages: pre-, beginning, mid-, advanced, and post-pubertal.

Table 2.1. Means for Pubertal Status and Socializing Messages by Gender

	Girls			Boys		
Variable	N	M	SD	N	M	SD
Pubertal status	189	2.80	0.84	146	2.75	0.79
		Mathematics				
Importance						
Female peers	189	2.08	0.58	141	1.97	0.65
Male peers	189	1.86	0.57	143	1.92	0.70
Perceived ability						
Female peers	185	3.08	0.67	142	2.90	0.84
Male peers	185	2.77	0.83	143	2.85	0.82
Career expectations						
Female peers	186	2.36	0.67	139	2.30	0.70
Male peers	186	2.16	0.71	141	2.29	0.70
Gender stereotypes						
Female peers	156	3.00	0.52	116	2.97	0.59
Male peers	154	2.83	0.46	116	2.82	0.59
		Social				
Importance						
Female peers	188	2.96	0.61	140	2.67	0.71
Male peers	188	2.49	0.77	142	2.52	0.66
Perceived ability						
Female peers	183	3.33	0.65	136	2.80	0.89
Male peers	183	3.07	0.83	138	2.74	0.88
Career expectations						
Female peers	187	2.75	0.71	139	2.39	0.76
Male peers	187	2.38	0.78	141	2.26	0.67
Gender stereotypes						
Female peers	162	3.58	0.54	121	3.36	0.72
Male peers	161	3.30	0.55	123	3.18	0.75

The distribution of categorical scores is summarized to provide a more descriptive portrait of the study sample's pubertal development. The vast majority of this sample reported being in either mid-, advanced, or post-pubertal stages (92 percent of girls and 82 percent of boys). Continuous and categorical scores were strongly correlated (rs = .93 for girls and boys).

Perceived Peer Gender Stereotypes. Adolescents' perceptions of peer gender stereotypes about each domain were assessed with fifteen-item scales; three components of domain value—interest value, utility value, and self-concept value (Eccles-Parsons et al., 1983)—were each measured with five items. Sample items included "How much do girls you know believe that girls and boys think relationships are interesting?" "How much do boys you know believe that girls and boys will use math in daily life?" and "How much do girls you know believe that girls and boys want to be good at caring for others because it is important for who they are as a person?"

Response options were on a 5-point scale: 1 = Boys a lot more than girls; 2 = Boys a little more than girls; 3 = About the same; 4 = Girls a little more than boys; and 5 = Girls a lot more than boys. Higher values for gender stereotypes indicate that the domain is perceived as more interesting and useful for girls than for boys; lower values indicate that the domain is more interesting and useful for boys than girls. Internal consistency alphas ranged from .93 to .94.

Perceived Peer Messages About Domain Importance for Adolescent. The achievement importance measure consisted of nine items for each domain. Sample items included "How important do boys you know think it is for you to be good at caring for others?" "How much do girls you know encourage you to be interested in math?" and "How much do boys you know expect you to be involved in math and math-related activities?" Response options were on a 4-point scale: 1 = Not at all; 2 = Not very; 3 = Somewhat; and 4 = Very. Internal consistency alphas ranged from .88 to .91.

Perceived Peer Messages About Adolescent Ability. Student report of peers' perceptions of their ability to achieve in social relationships and mathematics included such items as "How much do girls you know think that you are good at showing you care in relationships?" and "How much do boys you know think that you do well at math?" There were three items for each domain. Response options were on a 4-point scale: 1 = Not at all; 2 = Not much; 3 = Some; and 4 = A lot. Internal consistency alphas ranged from .86 to .87.

Perceived Peer Messages About Career Expectations for Adolescent. Adolescents were asked how much their peers thought they should work in jobs with particular characteristics. There were eight items for each domain. Items were based on the career counseling literature. In general, people in careers emphasizing math skills, such as scientists, engineers, and accountants, prefer to engage in different kinds of tasks than do people in careers emphasizing social skills, such as counselors, nurses, and teachers (Macdaid, McCaulley, & Kainz, 1991). Math domain items included "How much do girls you know think you should work in a job/career where you think of ideas to solve difficult problems?" Social domain items included "How much do boys you know think you should work in a job/career where you guide and teach others?" Response options were on a four-point scale: 1 = Not at all; 2 = Not much; 3 = Some; and 4 = A lot. Internal consistency alphas ranged from .87 to .89.

Analytic Model
SAS mixed procedure was used to examine puberty-related changes in adolescents' perceptions of peer messages. The analytic model included pubertal status (continuous score), gender (girls versus boys), and peer (female peers versus male peers). Peer was a repeated measure, and interactions among all independent variables were included in the model. Analyses excluded participants with a residual greater than three; only two variables

excluded more than two cases. Four pairs of dependent variables were examined: (1) math and social perceived peer *gender stereotypes*, (2) math and social perceived peer messages about domain *importance* for adolescent, (3) math and social perceived peer messages about adolescent *ability*, and (4) math and social perceived peer messages about *career expectations* for adolescent.

Examination of results focused on the slopes for the relation between pubertal development and the dependent variable. For gender stereotypes, a negative slope indicated that with pubertal maturation, adolescents felt that peers were placing greater value on the domain for boys relative to girls; a positive slope indicated perceived increases in the domain's value for girls relative to boys. For peer messages about the adolescent, a negative slope indicated that with pubertal maturation, adolescents perceived peer messages about the domain to be less encouraging; positive slopes indicated more encouraging messages. For these latter analyses, significant gender differences between slopes would be required to support the gender intensification hypothesis.

Results

Findings are discussed by domain.

Math Domain. As shown in Figure 2.1, findings supported my hypothesis that with pubertal maturation, adolescents would be increasingly likely to report that peers stereotyped math as more valuable for boys than girls (B = -0.11, p < .0001). The mean score changed from 3.12 to 2.78 from the earliest to latest pubertal stages. Examining mean scores across pubertal levels to determine where they differed from a value of 3.00, which represents equal domain value for girls and boys, I found that pre-pubertal adolescents perceived that peers thought math was of greater value for girls than boys, whereas mid-pubertal to post-pubertal adolescents thought math was of greater value for boys than girls. These areas are shaded in Figure 2.1.

Contrary to expectations, although the difference in girls' and boys' slopes was significant for male peer messages about math *importance* [t (325) = 2.50, *p* = .01], more advanced pubertal status among boys was associated with more negative perceptions of male peer math importance messages (*B* = -0.17, *p* = .008); girls' perceptions of these messages were not associated with pubertal status (*B* = 0.04, ns). For both boys and girls, female peer messages about math importance were perceived to decrease with pubertal maturation.

In addition, with pubertal maturation, adolescents reported more positive other-sex peer messages about math *ability* and more encouragement from both female and male peers to pursue math *careers*. Gender differences in these associations were not significant.

Figure 2.1. Perceived Peer Math Gender Stereotypes by Pubertal Status

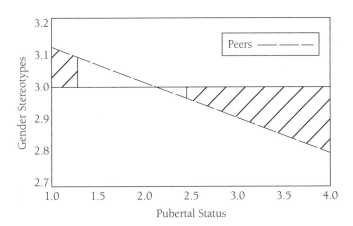

Social Domain. As shown in Figure 2.2, findings supported my hypothesis that with pubertal maturation, adolescents would be increasingly likely to report that female and male peers *stereotyped* the social domain as more valuable for girls than boys (Bs = 0.13 and 0.23 for female peers and male peers, respectively, ps < .002). From the earliest to latest pubertal stages, mean scores grew from 3.26 to 3.64 for female peers and from 2.89 to 3.57 for male peers. Examining mean scores across pubertal levels to determine where they differed from a value of 3.00, I found that adolescents of all pubertal levels perceived that female peers thought the social domain was of greater value for girls than boys, whereas adolescents in mid- to post-puberty perceived that male peers thought this. The area for male peers is shaded in Figure 2.2.

Consistent with expectations, the difference in girls' and boys' slopes was significant for male peer messages about social *careers* [t (322) = 2.60, p = .01], with more advanced pubertal status among girls associated with perceptions of more positive male peer social career messages (B = 0.32, p < .0001) and with boys' pubertal status being unrelated to their perceptions of these messages (B = 0.06, ns). At the end of puberty, girls, as compared to boys, perceived greater male peer expectations that they should work in careers emphasizing the social domain (Ms = 2.76 and 2.34 for girls and boys, respectively, p = .004). For both girls and boys, female peer encouragement of social careers was perceived to increase with pubertal level.

With pubertal maturation, adolescents of both genders perceived more positive peer messages about social *importance* and *ability*. Gender differences in these associations were not significant.

**Figure 2.2. Perceived Female and Male Peer Social Gender
Stereotypes by Pubertal Status**

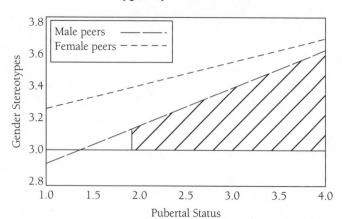

Discussion

Findings from the current study, based on adolescents' perceptions of peer messages, provide support for the existence of gender intensification of peer socialization in both math and social domains during puberty. Findings for peer gender stereotypes were more consistent than were those for peer messages about individual adolescents.

Perceived Peer Gender Stereotypes. As expected, with advances in pubertal status, adolescents increasingly perceived that peers thought math was of more value for boys than girls and thought the social domain was of more value for girls than boys. These findings have implications for adolescents' self-concept and career choices. In a study of women with doctoral degrees, male peers played a central role in communicating gender stereotypes about their professions, such as psychology and mathematics, and the women first noticed these stereotypes during adolescence (Boswell, 1985). In turn, if women choose careers inconsistent with female gender stereotypes, they may have to resist messages that they will not have the necessary abilities to succeed in their career and that they will face negative consequences for not conforming to gender stereotypes.

Perceived Peer Messages About the Individual Adolescent. Contrary to expectations, in the *math domain* there was no evidence for gender intensification of peer messages about the individual adolescent. Indeed, findings for perceived peer messages about math *importance* indicated declines for all adolescents, but particularly for boys. Whereas peers may recognize the importance of basic math skills learned at younger ages, they may be less likely to understand the importance of advanced math. Also, during the pubertal process adolescents may perceive a relative decline in peer messages about math importance because, as the number of new and distinct domains about which adolescents communicate grows, those messages come to represent a smaller proportion of peer messages. It is worthy of note that although inconsistent with the gender intensification hypothesis, greater declines in male peer math importance messages for boys, as compared to girls, are consistent with other work indicating that for older adolescent boys academic achievement is viewed as inconsistent with masculinity (Martino, 2000).

Although declines were found for peer messages about math importance, adolescents perceived increases in other-sex peer messages about math ability and careers. *Ability* findings may be the result of a combination of the increasing difficulty of math content and the growing awareness of the other sex during adolescence. As a result of gender segregation during childhood, early in puberty adolescents may know the relative ability of their same-sex but not other-sex peers. Later, adolescents may become increasingly aware of the abilities of the other sex, and, in the context of increasing math difficulty, this awareness may result in adolescents being impressed with the abilities of the other sex. Increases in math *career* messages may reflect a growing focus on careers in general among older adolescents.

In regard to the *social* domain, the growing focus on dating and peer friendships during adolescence is likely to explain the overall pattern of increases in perceived peer social messages—for both girls and boys—with pubertal maturation. The greater intensification of male peers' social *career* messages for girls, in combination with perceptions that peers, but particularly male peers, are increasingly thinking the social domain is of more value for girls than boys, may play an important role in pushing girls to attend more to this domain, perhaps especially so if girls are interested in heterosexual dating (Hill & Lynch, 1983).

Female Versus Male Peers. Results indicated that both female and male peers were perceived to participate in intensification of messages about math and social domain *gender stereotypes*. Male peers, but not female peers, were perceived to engage in gender intensification of messages about the *individual adolescent*. Perceptions of male peers' greater involvement in gender intensification may not be surprising given evidence that males' gender stereotypes tend to be more traditional than those of females, and males have more rigid gender proscriptions than females (Matlin, 1993).

Caveats. Although the findings from the current study provide some support for the gender intensification hypothesis, several notes of caution are necessary. First, the data come from a predominantly white, upper-middle-class sample, limiting their generalizability.

Second, the data are cross-sectional. Although participants were in schools that fed into one another, it would be preferable to obtain longitudinal data to reveal how adolescents' perceptions change during their own developmental course. A longitudinal design would also allow for examination of how variations in the pubertal process, such as in its timing and length, are related to one's experience of gender intensification.

Third, the data are based only on adolescents' reports of what their peers think. Although there are good reasons for assessing adolescents' perceptions (Hill & Lynch, 1983), it would be informative to obtain direct assessments from peers about the messages they give adolescents.

Fourth, self-report of pubertal status may have limitations. Medical professionals' ratings based on Tanner stages are considered the gold standard for measurement of puberty, although it is acknowledged that self-report measures are often the only practical option. The Pubertal Development Scale (Petersen, Crockett, Richards, & Boxer, 1988), used in this study, is considered to be an acceptable self-report measure for obtaining rough estimates of pubertal maturation (Alsaker, 1996; Coleman & Coleman, 2002). It also may be worthwhile to examine in future work whether there are cases in which adolescents' self-perceptions of their pubertal maturation may be more meaningful for explaining outcomes than their actual level (Alsaker, 1996). Other work might address whether accuracy of self-reported pubertal status is associated with the adolescent's gender or age, or the timing, sequence, or stage of various aspects of her or his pubertal maturation.

New Directions

The findings from the current study should stimulate renewed attention to the gender intensification hypothesis and its role in shaping adolescents' perceptions of and engagement in gender-related domains. There is already evidence to suggest that peer stereotypes and messages about the individual adolescent are associated with adolescents' own attitudes about math and social domains. Whether these attitudes in turn influence actual achievement-related choices has yet to be examined in a gender intensification framework. In addition to further exploration of the domains examined in the current study, examination of other domains will help detail the depth and breadth of gender intensification.

Examining the experience of gender intensification among adolescents of various ethnicities and socioeconomic classes is another worthwhile pursuit, particularly with regard to achievement domains. If expectations for achievement are raised or lowered for both female and male members of a particular class or ethnicity, the gender intensification hypothesis may not be relevant for explaining variations in engagement in achievement-related behaviors, although it may be relevant for other domains.

The current study also calls for renewed attention to the influence of male and female peers on adolescents' attitudes and behaviors. One direction to pursue would involve examination of how influential these messages are and for whom. Another direction meriting further exploration is the question of how and under what circumstances adolescents can resist messages that place limits on their development.

The importance of the social domain highlighted by the current study points to pursuing how boys can be encouraged to value and engage in relationally oriented thinking and behavior. This might be difficult work given the tendency for males to eschew female-associated behaviors and interests. Nonetheless, these efforts could guide the development of interventions that would serve to expand the range of domains in which both girls and boys consider achieving.

Finally, the intersection of math and social domains deserves further attention. Although findings from the current study suggest that some girls are no longer overtly discouraged from participating or achieving in mathematics, it may be that for many their gradual disengagement from mathematics during puberty is facilitated by perceptions that peers increasingly value and emphasize their involvement in the social domain. Girls may thus attend more to socially oriented activities at the expense of math and other domains that are not seen as compatible with or relevant to the social domain. Educational approaches that apply math and science to societal problems and social arenas should be examined in rigorous intervention studies to test their effectiveness at enhancing adolescents' engagement in math and science.

References

Alsaker, F. D. (1996). Annotation: The impact of puberty. *Journal of Child Psychology and Psychiatry, 37*, 249–258.

Blyth, D. A., & Traeger, C. (1988). Adolescent self-esteem and perceived relationships with parents and peers. In S. Salinger, J. Antrobus, & M. Hammer (Eds.), *Social networks of children, adolescents, and college students* (pp. 171–194). Mahwah, NJ: Erlbaum.

Boswell, S. L. (1985). The influence of sex-role stereotyping on women's attitudes and achievement in mathematics. In S. F. Chipman, L. R. Brush, & D. M. Wilson (Eds.), *Women and mathematics: Balancing the equation* (pp.175–198). Mahwah, NJ: Erlbaum.

Brown, B. B. (1990). Peer groups and peer cultures. In S. S. Feldman & G. R. Elliot (Eds.), *At the threshold: The developing adolescent* (pp. 171–196). Cambridge, MA: Harvard University Press.

Center for Early Adolescence. (1984, Summer). Girls, math, and science. *Issues in Middle-Grade Education: Research and Resources*, pp. 1–7.

Coleman, L., & Coleman, J. (2002). The measurement of puberty: A review. *Journal of Adolescence, 25*, 535–550.

Eccles, J. (1989). Bringing young women to math and science. In M. Crawford & M. Gentry (Eds.), *Gender and thought: Psychological perspectives* (pp. 36–58). New York: Springer-Verlag.

Eccles-Parsons, J., Adler, T. F., Futterman, R., Goff, S. B., Kaczala, C. M., Meece, J. L., & Midgley, C. (1983). Expectancies, values, and academic behaviors. In J. T. Spence (Ed.), *Achievement and achievement motives: Psychological and sociological approaches* (pp. 75–146). San Francisco: Freeman.

Fechner, P. Y. (2002). Gender differences in puberty. *Journal of Adolescent Health, 30*(4), Suppl. 1, 44–48.

Galambos, N. L., Almeida, D. M., & Petersen, A. C. (1990). Masculinity, femininity, and sex role attitudes in early adolescence: Exploring gender intensification. *Child Development, 61*, 1905–1914.

Hill, J. P., & Lynch, M. E. (1983). The intensification of gender-related role expectations during early adolescence. In J. Brooks-Gunn & A. Petersen (Eds.), *Girls at puberty: Biological and psychosocial perspectives* (pp. 201–228). New York: Plenum Press.

Hyde, J. S., Fennema, E., & Lamon, S. J. (1990). Gender differences in mathematics performance: A meta-analysis. *Psychological Bulletin, 107,* 139–155.

Hyde, J. S., Fennema, E., Ryan, M., Frost, L. A., & Hopp, C. (1990). Gender comparisons of mathematics attitudes and affect: A meta-analysis. *Psychology of Women Quarterly, 14,* 299–324.

Jacobs, J. E., & Eccles, J. S. (1992). The impact of mothers' gender-role stereotypic beliefs on mothers' and children's ability perceptions. *Journal of Personality and Social Psychology, 63,* 932–944.

Leaper, C. (1994). Exploring the consequences of gender segregation on social relationships. In C. Leaper (Ed.), *Childhood gender segregation: Causes and consequences,* New Directions for Child Development, no. 65, pp. 67–86.

Lytton, H., & Romney, D. M. (1991). Parents' differential socialization of boys and girls: A meta-analysis. *Psychological Bulletin, 109,* 267–296.

Macdaid, G. P., McCaulley, M. H., & Kainz, R. I. (1991). *Myers-Briggs type indicator: Atlas of type tables.* Gainesville, FL: Center for Applications of Psychological Type.

Martino, W. (2000). Mucking around in class, giving crap, and acting cool: Adolescent boys enacting masculinities at school. *Canadian Journal of Education, 25,* 102–112.

Matlin, M. W. (1993). *The psychology of women.* Orlando: Harcourt.

Petersen, A. C., Crockett, L., Richards, M., & Boxer, A. (1988). A self-report measure of pubertal status: Reliability, validity, and initial norms. *Journal of Youth and Adolescence, 17,* 117–133.

Pettitt, L. M. (2001, April). *Pubertal development, perceptions of parents' and peers' beliefs, and adolescents' gender stereotypes about math and relationships.* Paper presented at the biennial meeting of the Society for Research in Child Development, Minneapolis, MN.

Stipp, D. (1992, September 11). The gender gap: Our schools make it hard for girls to pursue math and science. *The Wall Street Journal, p. B8.*

LISA M. PETTITT *is senior instructor in the Department of Pediatrics at the University of Colorado Health Sciences Center.*

3

Teachers and peers have a unique impact on Latino students' math and science perceptions and performance.

Parents, Teachers, and Peers: Discrepant or Complementary Achievement Socializers?

Heather A. Bouchey

Despite considerable knowledge of the processes underlying successful academic performance (see Eccles, Wigfield, & Schiefele, 1998), our understanding of the connections between inter- and intrapersonal achievement mechanisms remains limited. Scholars in educational and developmental psychology have established a broad base of empirical findings concerning the student-level characteristics and capacities that predict academic performance (see Wigfield & Eccles, 2002; Aronson, 2002). We also know that significant others' beliefs and behaviors regarding academics predict student performance (see Juvonen & Wentzel, 1996; Wigfield & Harold, 1992). However, research on the *interplay* between others' influence and students' own psychological factors in predicting achievement merits considerably more theoretical and empirical attention (Wentzel, 1999).

One theoretical framework that simultaneously incorporates both socializing agents' beliefs and the individual's self-perception system is symbolic interactionism (Cooley, 1902; Mead, 1934). According to symbolic interaction theory (SIT), the individual forms "reflected appraisals" of what others think of him or her, which are in turn used to construct the individual's own self-concept. When others think highly of an individual, he or she is presumed to recognize this positive regard from others and subsequently

This research was supported by an American Psychological Association dissertation research grant awarded to Heather A. Bouchey and by NIH Grant R01 HD 09613, awarded to Susan Harter.

construct a positive self-image. This model is predicated on the fact that the individual's reflected appraisals are an accurate representation of "reality" in the form of others' beliefs.

We have previously found support for the application of SIT to the academic domain (Bouchey & Harter, 2004). A series of SEM analyses with cross-sectional data revealed that early adolescents' perceptions of parents' and teachers' academic beliefs and behavior predicted students' own achievement beliefs and behavior, which in turn predicted their school performance. Although these previous analyses provided empirical support for the second component of SIT (that is, that there are links among students' reflected appraisals and their own self-perceptions), the extent to which significant others' actual reports correspond to students' reflected appraisals of others' beliefs and behavior was not examined. I explore these relations in the present chapter.

Perceived Ability, Importance, and Support

In the past several decades, perceived ability and importance have emerged as central predictors of academic performance. A considerable body of evidence indicates that both the extent to which children (1) feel academically competent and (2) believe that it is important to do well in school predict their subsequent performance, course choices, and academic plans (Eccles et al., 1998; Fuligni, 1997; Harter, 1998, 1999; Marsh, 1990). In addition, the degree to which *parents* report that their child is competent and that it is important for their child to do well in school predicts his or her achievement and performance (Eccles-Parsons, Adler, & Kaczala, 1982; Phillips, 1987). Moreover, teachers' views of individual students' ability can create a powerful self-fulfilling prophecy, both directly and indirectly affecting children's school performance (Rosenthal, 2002; Rosenthal & Jacobson, 1968; Madon et al., 2001; Wigfield & Harold, 1992). To date, we understand less about the extent to which teachers' and classmates' beliefs regarding how important it is for particular students to do well in specific courses influence students' own importance beliefs and performance.

In addition to significant others' beliefs, the *behaviors* that they engage in are linked to students' academic outcomes. For instance, the extent to which significant others provide both instrumental and emotional support predicts students' scholastic success. Pratt, Green, MacVicar, and Bountrogianni (1992) demonstrated that maternal scaffolding of effective math problem solving was associated with enhanced math achievement in fifth graders. Emotional support from parents, teachers, and peers is positively related to young adolescents' expectancies for doing well, valuing of academics, academic engagement, perceived competence, and performance (Furrer & Skinner, 2003; Gonzalez, Cauce, Friedman, & Mason, 1996; Goodnow, 1993; Harter & Robinson, 1988; Wentzel, 1998). One limitation of many previous studies is a reliance on rather global indices of support, rather than on support linked specifically to performance in particular coursework.

In this study, I tested the model depicted in Figure 3.1. Basing my hypotheses on prior research and SIT, I expected parents', teachers', and classmates' beliefs regarding the *importance* of math and science and the individual student's *ability* in math and science to predict students' reflected appraisals of others' beliefs. In turn, I hypothesized that students' reflected appraisals would predict their own self-perceptions, scholastic behavior, and math and science performance. Support from others was also expected to predict students' reflected appraisals, as illustrated in Figure 3.1. To rule out the alternative hypothesis that students' previous academic performance accounted for relations among significant others' perceptions, students' reflected appraisals, self-perceptions, and current performance, I also controlled for students' previous achievement.

Similarity or Dissimilarity in Socializers' Effects?

Do different social partners influence achievement outcomes in the same way? In the preceding section, I reviewed findings concerning parental, teacher, and peer effects on achievement and scholastic performance. However, the majority of previous investigations have focused on parents, teachers, *or* peers as socializing agents. What happens if the effects of these three social partners are *simultaneously* examined?

We might expect that parents, teachers, and peers function as *complementary* socializers, wherein patterns of influence are similar for all three sets of social partners. For instance, emotional support from each of these interaction partners predicts academic engagement and motivation (Furrer & Skinner, 2003; Wentzel, 1998). Alternatively, we might predict that the influence of parents, teachers, and peers is *distinct* or *discrepant* from one another, especially with respect to phenomena such as ability beliefs or the perceived importance of schoolwork. For instance, it is possible that adults (parents and teachers) are important socializers of students' beliefs about the importance of particular coursework, whereas peers are not. On the other hand, peers have recently been hypothesized to have a particularly salient effect on youths' valuing of school and coursework (Fordham & Ogbu, 1986; Steinberg, 1996), suggesting that their impact on the valuing of academics may be greater than that of adults. Yet another prediction is that *school* socializers (teachers and classmates) have a stronger impact on individual students' academic beliefs and behaviors than do family members.

Following the tradition of previous research that demonstrates different patterns for the effects of parents, teachers, and peers on mathematics achievement (Ma, 2001), future academic expectations (Colarossi, 2000), and academic goal orientations (Wentzel, 1998), I examined the extent to which socialization patterns for these three sets of social partners were similar or different. A novel contribution of this study concerns the examination

Figure 3.1. Conceptual Model for Study

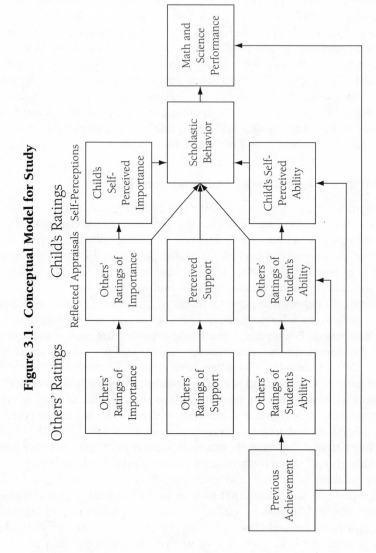

of parental, peer, and teacher influence with respect to the *same* achievement processes or mechanisms. It is possible that previous research on achievement socialization revealed differences among social partners because investigators were examining different types of processes for different partners. Although this approach is certainly meaningful and informative, it does not sufficiently capture whether parents, teachers, and peers function as complementary versus discrepant socializers. By examining the same socialization constructs for each of these three social partners, I hoped to capture similarities and differences that would not be confounded by looking at different processes. I investigated the extent to which these social partners exerted similar or dissimilar influence[1] with respect to the *importance* of math and science, their *support* for doing well in math and science, and their beliefs regarding the target student's *ability* in math and science (see Figure 3.1). Due to the relative lack of previous research in this area, I did not generate a priori hypotheses about the nature of such similarity or dissimilarity.

Math and Science Achievement in Latino Youth

The current study presented a unique opportunity to investigate achievement socialization processes and math and science performance in Latino youth. This feature is important for several reasons. First, U.S. students continue to underachieve in math and science as compared to their age mates from other nations (Fuligni & Stevenson, 1995; National Commission on Mathematics and Science Teaching for the 21st Century, 2000). This consistent pattern highlights the need to fully understand achievement processes for these particular courses. Moreover, relatively few studies to date have examined math and science achievement socialization in Latino populations, despite the fact that Latinos are (on average) more likely to underperform and less likely to strive toward future careers in these domains than are European Americans (see Ginorio & Huston, 2001; Peng, Wright, & Hill, 1995). Given demographic predictions of increasing numbers of Latinos residing in the United States during the next several decades (for example, McLoyd, 1998), it is crucial to explore the processes underlying math and science achievement in this population.

With this ultimate goal in mind, I thus examined mean-level differences between Latino and European American students in parents', teachers', and peers' reports of their instrumental and emotional support for math and science, the importance of math and science for each target student, and his or her ability in these courses. Given the previously proposed links between significant others' beliefs and behavior and students' own self-perceptions, I expected this set of analyses to shed light on why Latino students consistently demonstrate poorer math and science performance as compared to European American students. To avoid confounding ethnicity with socioeconomic status (see Graham, 1994), I statistically controlled for the effects of maternal educational level.

Method

Participants Participants included 378 students, 150 mothers, and 21 teachers from two public middle schools in the metropolitan Denver area; 70 percent of the students in these two schools qualified for free or reduced meals (Denver Public Schools Information Line, [MDJ1]1998). Females constituted 53 percent of the sample, which comprised 46 percent sixth-grade students, 32 percent seventh graders, and 22 percent eighth graders. Students were primarily Latino (65 percent) and European American (21 percent). A small proportion of participating students (11 percent) attended English as a Second Language (ESL) classes. Teachers deemed each of these students proficient enough in English to participate in the study. The majority of students (54 percent) had married parents; 51 percent of the students reported that their mothers had a high school diploma or less education.

Procedure Of the recruited students, 72 percent obtained parental consent to participate. Students and teachers completed questionnaires in their classrooms during regularly scheduled classes of fifty to sixty minutes in duration. Questionnaires for all students and teachers were administered in English. Parent questionnaires were completed at home, in the language (English or Spanish) in which parents had completed informed consent forms. Of the mothers who agreed to participate, 51 percent mailed back completed questionnaires.

Measures Socializers' beliefs and behavior, adolescents' reflected appraisals, and adolescents' own beliefs and behavior were assessed with self-report questionnaires. All self-report measures employed 4-point ratings ranging from "Not at all true" to "Very true." Both positively and negatively worded items were included in each questionnaire. All scales exhibited acceptable reliability ($\alpha > .70$), unless otherwise noted. Grades and prior achievement test scores from school records were also obtained.

Mothers' Beliefs and Behavior. Maternal perceptions of how important it was for their child to do well in math and science[2] and of their child's ability in math and science were assessed with modifications of Academic subscale items from the "How Important These Things Are" (seven items) and "What I Am Like" (five items) scales of the Self-Perception Profile for Adolescents (Harter, 1988). Sample items included "As a parent, I think it is very important for my child to do well in math/science" and "My child is pretty slow at finishing work in math/science." Mothers also completed a ten-item scale adapted from the Social Support Scale for Older Children and Adolescents (Harter & Robinson, 1988). Sample items included "I am proud of my son's/daughter's grades in math/science" and "I don't teach my son/daughter about the things he/she wants to know in math/science."

Teachers' Beliefs and Behavior. Due to the large sample size of this study, it was impractical to ask math and science teachers to complete separate full-length questionnaires for each of the participating students. Thus, teacher ratings of the importance of math and science schoolwork for each student and his or her ability were assessed with two items: "It is important for this student to do well in *math* [or *science*]" and "This student is smart and can do work quickly in *math* [or *science*]." Math and science teachers' ratings were averaged to yield overall measures of teachers' perceived importance and ability for each student. One-item ratings of approval and instrumental support for each student were also obtained. To maintain consistency with parent and classmate measures, these ratings were averaged across support type and teachers to yield a global support score for math and science teachers.

Classmates' Beliefs and Behavior. Classmate ratings of importance, ability, and support were assessed with measures very similar to those used with teachers. However, the classmate items combined math and science courses together. In addition, because a number of classmates (*n* = 8 to 28) responded for each student, I computed average classmate ratings of importance, ability, and support for each student in the sample.

Reflected Appraisals of Importance and Ability. Adolescents' perceptions of others' beliefs regarding the importance of doing well in math and science schoolwork and their perceptions of others' beliefs about his or her academic ability were measured with modifications of the "How Important These Things Are" (seven items) and "What I Am Like" (five items) scales of the Self-Perception Profile for Adolescents (Harter, 1988). All items asked students about mothers, parents, and classmates separately. Sample items include "My *mother* [teacher, classmates] think(s) it is very important for me to do well in math/science" and "My *mother* [teacher, classmates] think(s) I am pretty slow at finishing work in math/science."

Reflected Appraisals of Support. Students' perceived support for math and science schoolwork was assessed with an adaptation of the Social Support Scale for Older Children and Adolescents (Harter & Robinson, 1988). Five items from both the Approval Support and Instrumental Support subscales were modified to reflect support specifically tailored to math and science. I created average global ratings of adolescents' perceived math and science support from mothers, teachers, and classmates.

Perceived Importance and Ability. Adolescents' perceptions of the importance of math and science schoolwork and their ability in these courses were assessed using modifications of "How Important These Things Are" (seven items) and "What I Am Like" (five items) scales of the Self-Perception Profile for Adolescents (Harter, 1988). Sample items included "It is very important for me to do well in math/science" and "I think I am pretty slow at finishing work in math/science."

Scholastic Behavior. Adolescents' time and energy devoted to math and science were assessed with a novel seven-item measure. Sample items included "I make sure that I get to math/science class on time" and "I probably don't spend enough time working on homework in math/science."

Current Performance. Students' current marking period grades were obtained from school records. Letter grades for math and science classes were converted to a 13-point scale (for example, A+ = 12, C- = 4, F = 0) and were averaged to generate a math and science performance score for each student.

Prior Achievement. Students' achievement test scores from the previous spring (one year before this study) were also obtained from school records. Percentile ranks from math and science subtests of the Iowa Test of Basic Skills were averaged to measure previous achievement.

Results

A series of path analyses were conducted to test the mediational role of adolescents' reflected appraisals and whether models were similar for mothers, teachers, and classmates. In addition, ANOVAs were run to examine mean-level differences in socializers' beliefs and behavior by ethnic group.

Reflected Appraisals as Mediators. Contrary to my predictions based on SIT, students' reflected appraisals of others' beliefs and behavior did not function as mediators between significant others' actual beliefs and students' own academic self-perceptions. To examine this set of hypotheses, I conducted three separate path analyses with parents', teachers,' or peers' reports of the importance of doing well in math and science, the extent to which they provided support in these courses, and their perceptions of the target student's ability in math and science; students' reflected appraisals of the social partners' beliefs and behaviors; and students' own perceived importance of doing well in math and science, ability in these courses, and the extent to which they engaged in good study practices (see Figure 3.1).

Acceptable fit indices were obtained for all three of these analyses with the reflected self-appraisals as mediators in the model. However, these patterns of good fit could have been a statistical artifact due to increased model complexity (see Kline, 1998). Thus it was important to demonstrate that including the reflected appraisals improved the model fit above and beyond that obtained when only others' reports and students' self-perceptions were included in the model. This did not occur. I obtained an equivalent fit for both the less complex and more complex models, and was thus forced to accept the more parsimonious models. Thus there was no evidence that students' perceptions of what others thought and did functioned as crucial mediators between what others reported and students' own self-perceptions.

Similarity and Dissimilarity in Socialization Processes. Separate path analyses for mothers, teachers, and peers revealed patterns of both similarity across social partners and distinct relations, depending on the construct. For teachers, their ratings of both how important it was for a particular student to do well in math and science and how capable the student was in math and science predicted students' corresponding self-perceptions, which in turn predicted their behavior and performance (see Figure 3.2). However, teachers' ratings of support were *not* related to either students' self-perceptions or their academic behavior. In addition, teachers' reports of how much support they provided were not significantly correlated with the students' perceived support from teachers ($r = .10$, $p = .07$), suggesting a mismatch between what teachers and students believed was happening in the classroom. In contrast, students' and classmates' reports concerning support were positively related ($r = .21$, $p < .001$).

Mothers' perceptions of their child's ability were linked to his or her own perceived ability, consistent with the pattern for teachers. Unlike those of teachers, however, mothers' beliefs regarding how important math and science were for their child were not linked to the students' own perceived importance of doing well in these courses. The best-fitting model for mothers also included their support ratings, but their reports of support were not significantly linked with any of the children's self-perceptions (see Figure 3.3).

Peer ratings of importance were not linked to individual students' self-perceived importance (a pattern similar to that for mothers). However, levels of peer support did (positively) predict the extent to which children engaged in good study and school practices (see Figure 3.4). This was a pattern unique to peers in that support from neither mothers nor teachers was a significant predictor of students' scholastic behavior. Similar to the models for both mothers and teachers, peers' ratings of each student's ability predicted his or her own perceived ability. Interestingly, the best-fitting model for peers also included a bidirectional relation between peers' ratings of support and the target student's ability.

Mean-Level Differences in Socializers' Beliefs and Behavior. The third research question concerned mean-level ethnic differences in socializers' reports of importance, support, and ability for target children. To examine this, I employed analyses of variance with student's ethnic group (Latino or European American) entered as the independent variable and mothers', teachers', and peers' importance, support, or ability ratings entered as dependent variables.[3] I covaried out the effect of maternal education in all analyses in which it was related to the outcome.

With respect to the importance of doing well in math and science, Latino mothers ($M = 3.94$, $SD = .15$) reported that it was more important for their child to do well in these subjects than did European American mothers ($M = 3.83$, $SD = .23$), $F(1, 118) = 8.91$, $p < .01$; eta-squared = .07. The opposite pattern was found for teachers, who indicated that it was more important for European American students ($M = 3.80$, $SD = .49$) to do well in math and science than Latino students ($M = 3.49$, $SD = .69$), $F(1, 284) = 12.25$, $p < .01$; eta-squared = .04. This is important given that teachers' ratings for importance predicted students' own ratings for the sample as a whole (recall from the path analyses).

An opposite pattern emerged for teacher and peer support for math and science. Whereas teachers reported providing more support for European American students (adj $M = 3.98$, $SE = .04$) than Latino students [(adj $M = 3.86$, $SE = .02$), $F(1, 197) = 7.04$, $p < .01$; eta-squared = .04], classmates

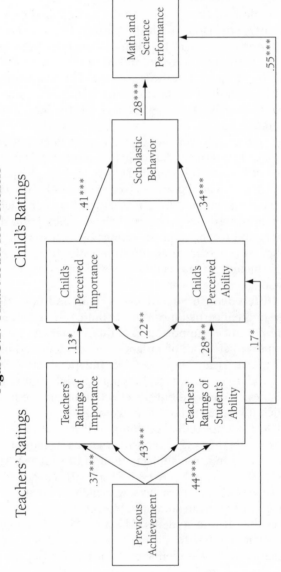

Figure 3.2. Final Model for Teachers

Note: X^2 (9) = 21.85, $p < .01$; CFI = .95; NNFI = .95; RMSEA = .07 (90% CI = 0.03, .12

*$p < .05$. **$p < .01$. ***$p < .001$

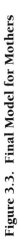
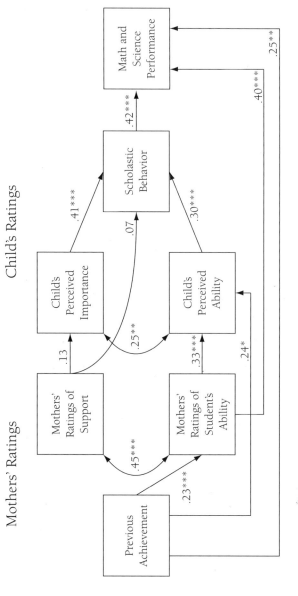

Figure 3.3. Final Model for Mothers

Mothers' Ratings

Child's Ratings

Previous Achievement

Mothers' Ratings of Support

Mothers' Ratings of Student's Ability

Child's Perceived Importance

Child's Perceived Ability

Scholastic Behavior

Math and Science Performance

.45***

.23***

.13

.33***

.24*

.25**

.07

.41***

.30***

.42***

.40***

.25**

Note: X^2 (6) = 7.31, *p* = .29; CFI = .99; NNFI = .98; RMSEA = .04 (90% CI = 0.00, .15)
p < .05. **p* < .01. ***p* < .001

Figure 3.4. Final Model for Classmates

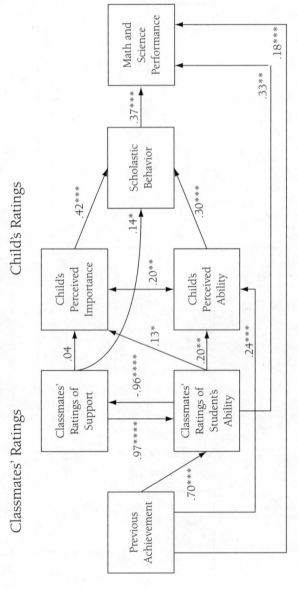

Note: X^2 (7) = 11.06, *p* = .14; CFI = .99; NNFI = .97; RMSEA = .05 (90% CI = 0.00, .10)

*p < .05. **p < .01. ** p < .001

reported providing more support for Latino students [(adj M = 2.49, SE = .03; for European Americans, adj M = 2.01, SE = .06), $F(1, 197)$ = 48.00, p <.001; eta-squared = .20]. Also, maternal education was related to classmate support, with higher maternal education correlated with less support (r = −.24, p < .001). Thus it appeared that the less well-off children (even within the Latino group) were getting more support from classmates, whereas European American children were getting more support from teachers.

Both teachers and peers reported that Latino students (M = 3.15, SD = .77, for teachers; M = 2.92, SD = .44, for peers) were less capable in math and science than European American students (M = 3.46, SD = .64, for teachers; M = 3.13, SD = .54, for peers) [for teachers $F(1, 274)$ = 9.6, p <.01, eta-squared = .03; for peers, $F(1, 274)$ = 11.02, p <.01, eta-squared = .04]. This was interesting both because teachers' and classmates' beliefs predicted children's own ability beliefs (recall from the path analyses) and because once the effects of maternal education were controlled for, Latino and European American students did *not* differ in terms of their math and science performance (p = .21).

Discussion

The primary goal of this investigation was to document that students' perceptions of what social partners think and do regarding math and science function as an important bridge between others' actual beliefs and behavior and students' own beliefs and behavior. This finding would lend support to the symbolic interactionist view of self-concept development, as applied to the academic domain. However, the results did not fully confirm SIT. Whereas I had previously found that students' perceptions of significant others regarding math and science predict their own corresponding self-perceptions and performance (Bouchey & Harter, 2004), the findings reported here indicate that students' reflected appraisals do not function as crucial mediators between social partners' actual perceptions (as reported via questionnaires) and students' self-perceptions. How can we make sense of this mixed support for SIT?

Prior empirical studies have demonstrated that parental views of children's academic ability are related to children's reflected appraisal beliefs (Eccles-Parsons et al., 1982; Felson, 1989), but I failed to replicate this association in the current study. Mothers', teachers', and peers' beliefs and support were not strongly related to students' perceptions of these beliefs and support, likely accounting for the fact that the path models fit well without reflected appraisals functioning as mediators. There are a number of possible explanations that could account for this noncorrespondence.

First, evidence indicates that adults and classmates may not be *accurate* reporters of children's competence and personality traits (Miller & Davis, 1992). In fact, in the Miller and Davis study mothers and teachers were better at predicting cognitive performance for a hypothetical "average" child than for the individual target child. Although these findings most closely relate to perceived ability in the current study, they raise the question of whether significant others' perceptions of importance and support may also be inaccurate.

It is also possible that the adolescents in this study were inaccurate. They may have incorrectly estimated parents', peers', and teachers' perceptions. Individuals may have difficulty assessing what others believe, particularly in the absence of explicit communication of this information (Cook & Douglas, 1998). For instance, it is unlikely that parents or teachers would *overtly* devalue the importance of math or science. Rather, they may *subtly* advance messages about the value of these courses by encouraging math and science activities or focusing on students' achievement in other domains, such as sports (see Eccles, 1993; Jacobs & Bleeker, this volume; Meece, Parsons, Kaczala, Goff, & Futterman, 1982). To the extent that adolescents are unaware of these more subtle processes, they may be unable to accurately report on others' actual views.

Finally, over time parents and children may become less attentive to the information they each provide regarding how they perceive each other (Kenny & DePaulo, 1993). It is possible that by early adolescence parents and children may be operating under rather outdated perceptions of each other's capabilities and views. Similar processes may also occur from the beginning to the end of the school year with teachers and classmates.

What do the current findings contribute with respect to SIT and the socialization of children's academic beliefs? They suggest that at least one component of SIT may be inaccurate. However, it is important to point out that this study adopted a "snapshot" approach to examine links among others' academic beliefs and behavior and students' corresponding beliefs and behavior. It is entirely possible that the middle school years are the wrong time frame for capturing these links. Perhaps the links occur, but at a much earlier time in development. By early adolescence, what is most important in predicting students' own self-perceptions may not be what significant others actually believe and do at any given time point, but rather what adolescents *think* others believe and do. This would fit with the cognitive egocentrism, characterized by an imaginary audience, that adolescents typically experience (see Elkind, 1985). However, even if it is true that adolescents' reflected appraisals predict academic self-perceptions, several questions remain unanswered. Where do reflected appraisals come from? Are they merely epiphenomena linked to broader changes in self-concept? We know that children's own self-perceptions become more abstract, differentiated, and multifaceted across time (see Harter, 1999). How does the emergence of reflected appraisals fit in with this process? Only longitudinal investigation can fully address these questions.

Above and beyond support for SIT, the second goal of this study was to investigate the extent to which different social partners exert similar versus dissimilar patterns of "influence" with respect to math and science achievement. This was an important goal given that most previous studies of achievement socialization have focused on only one or two social partners and have typically examined different mechanisms for different social partners. Overall, the results of this study revealed both complementary and divergent patterns, depending on the construct or "mechanism" in question.

In terms of ability beliefs, a complementary pattern for mothers, teachers, and classmates emerged. On average, each of these social partners' perceptions of the target student's ability in math and science was positively predictive of the student's own perceived ability. The relations held even after controlling for the effects of students' previous achievement in these courses. Indeed, it may be easier for parents, teachers, peers, and students themselves to be "on the same page" regarding a target student's ability because overt indicators, such as grades or classroom performance, are salient cues accessible to all.

In contrast to the pattern revealed for ability beliefs, discrepant patterns were revealed for the perceived importance of math and science and support. Teachers' views of the importance of math and science for a particular student, but not mothers' or peers' views, were related to the student's own importance perceptions. Although the measurement difficulties with mothers' importance beliefs in this study precluded a conclusive test of their effects, the findings indicate that peers do not have an impact on students' valuing of specific coursework. Rather, middle school students may look to their teachers for specific information about whether they should strive to excel in math and science, but look to their peers for messages about the overall value of school. The findings in this study thus have particular relevance for those interested in designing enrichment programs that promote students' interest in science and engineering. Although some existing programs rely on peer interactions to promote science interest (see Linn & Hsi, 2000), teachers may be more influential socializing agents, given their demonstrated capacity in this study to help students both identify the personal value of science and internalize that value.

A discrepant pattern of findings was also revealed for support in math and science. In this study, only *classmates'* support was a positive predictor of students' scholastic behavior. Support from neither mothers nor teachers was linked to students' scholastic behavior. This pattern is interesting given that the peer group does become more salient during early adolescence. The findings suggest that increased opportunities to interact scholastically with peers during middle school, and in particular to work together on tasks that foster instrumental and emotional support, would better enhance students' *independent* behavior in math and science. This model is quite different from the teacher-focused one typically adopted in middle school classrooms today (see Eccles et al., 1993). It is also interesting that the levels of support teachers reported providing were not related to students' perceived support from teachers. Precisely why this "mismatch" occurred between teachers' self-report and students' perceived support should be examined in future studies.

The final goal of this study was to examine mean-level differences in social partners' beliefs and behavior, in an effort to further elucidate why Latino students typically underperform in math and science as compared to their European American classmates. Overall, findings did shed light on the correlational patterns discussed earlier. In particular, teachers reported perceptions that unilaterally favored European American students in terms of importance, support, and ability in math and science, and classmates reported perceptions that favored European American students in terms of ability in math and science. The ethnicity-based distinctions made by teachers and classmates held even after the effects of socioeconomic status (SES) were controlled for. Particularly striking was the finding that teachers and classmates (most of whom were Latino) believed that Latino students were not as capable in math and science as European American students, even though the two groups did not differ in math and science grades once SES was controlled. These findings are consistent with those of Graham and colleagues (Graham, Taylor, & Hudley, 1998; Hudley & Graham, 2001), who demonstrated that classmates hold negative academic stereotypes about African American and Latino youth (particularly boys). The fact that the pattern favoring European American youth was even more pronounced for teachers in the current study indicates that additional research on the impact of negative stereotypes on minority adolescents' importance and ability beliefs, as well as on scholastic behaviors, is timely and necessary.

New Directions

This study theoretically and empirically integrated a set of intra- and interpersonal components underlying middle school students' performance in math and science. I attempted to capture "real world" processes by simultaneously investigating different social partners, and I also identified a possible *mechanism* (reflected appraisals) through which the social realm influences the student's inner world of academic self-perceptions. Additional investigations that focus on achievement *process*, rather than on descriptions of the correlates of academic outcomes, are most likely to push the field of achievement socialization forward. Instead of documenting *whether* significant others' perceptions and behaviors are linked to students' achievement (we know that they are), we need to focus on *how* these constructs become connected (we know much less about this aspect of achievement socialization). Such an approach would necessarily involve the collection of longitudinal data to explore developmental trajectories in mechanisms, focus on multiple social partners and their influence, and adequately capture both individual and dyadic or group processes. This approach would lead to further refinement of both individual-based processes and socialization processes, as well as the integration of both. Through the systematic identification and empirical validation of specific mechanisms (both implicit and explicit) linking the external and internal worlds of children, as well as individual differences in these mechanisms, we can begin to fully understand how to maximize scholastic success for all students.

Notes

1. Although causal relations cannot be established in the present study, the use of "influence" is consistent with the SIT framework.
2. Cronbach alpha reliability for this scale was .45. The reliability did not significantly improve after recomputing this scale without low-correlating items. I opted to leave this measure in for theoretical purposes.
3. To increase power, I ran separate ANCOVAs for mothers ($n = 120$) and MANCOVAs with teachers and peers together ($n = 199$ to 285).

References

Aronson, J. (Ed.). (2002). *Improving academic achievement: Impact of psychological factors on education.* Orlando: Academic Press.

Bouchey, H. A., & Harter, S. (2004). *Reflected appraisals, academic self-perceptions, and math/science achievement during early adolescence.* Manuscript submitted for publication.

Colarossi, L. G. (2000). *Gender differences in social support from parents, teachers, and peers: Implications for adolescent development.* Unpublished doctoral dissertation, University of Michigan.

Cook, W. L., & Douglas, E. M. (1998). The looking-glass self in family context: A social relations analysis. *Journal of Family Psychology, 12,* 299–309.

Cooley, C. H. (1902). *Human nature and the social order.* New York: Scribner.

Denver Public Schools Information Line. (1998).

Eccles, J. S. (1993). School and family effects on the ontogeny of children's interests, self-perceptions, and activity choice. In J. Jacobs (Ed.), *Nebraska symposium on motivation* (Vol. 14, pp. 145–208). Lincoln: University of Nebraska Press.

Eccles, J. S., Midgley, C., Wigfield, A., Buchanan, C. M., Reuman, D., Flanagan, C., & MacIver, D. (1993). Development during adolescence: The impact of stage-environment fit on young adolescents' experiences in schools and in families. *American Psychologist, 48,* 90–101.

Eccles, J. S., Wigfield, A., & Schiefele, U. (1998). Motivation to succeed. In W. Damon (Series Ed.) & N. Eisenberg (Vol. Ed.), *Handbook of child psychology: Vol. 3. Social, emotional, and personality development* (5th ed., pp. 1018–1095). New York: Wiley.

Eccles-Parsons, J., Adler, T. F., & Kaczala, C. M. (1982). Socialization of achievement attitudes and beliefs: Parental influences. *Child Development, 53,* 310–321.

Elkind, D. (1985). Egocentrism redux. *Developmental Review, 5,* 218–226.

Felson, R. B. (1989). Parents and the reflected appraisal process: A longitudinal analysis. *Journal of Personality and Social Psychology, 56,* 965–971.

Fordham, S., & Ogbu, J. U. (1986). Black students' school success: Coping with the "burden of acting white." *Urban Review, 18,* 176–206.

Fuligni, A. J. (1997). The academic achievement of adolescents from immigrant families: The roles of family background, attitudes, and behavior. *Child Development, 68,* 351–363.

Fuligni, A. J., & Stevenson, H. W. (1995). Time use and mathematics achievement among American, Chinese, and Japanese high school students. *Child Development, 66,* 830–842.

Furrer, C., & Skinner, E. (2003). Sense of relatedness as a factor in children's academic engagement and performance. *Journal of Educational Psychology, 95,* 148–162.

Ginorio, A., & Huston, M. (2001). *Si, se puede! Yes, we can: Latinas in school.* Washington, DC: American Association of University Women Educational Foundation.

Gonzalez, N. A., Cauce, A. M., Friedman, R. J., & Mason, C. A. (1996). Family, peer, and neighborhood influences on academic achievement among African-American adolescents: One-year prospective effects. *American Journal of Community Psychology, 24,* 365–387.

Goodnow, C. (1993). Classroom belonging among early adolescent students: Relationships to motivation and achievement. *Journal of Early Adolescence, 13,* 21–43.

Graham, S. (1994). Motivation in African Americans. *Review of Educational Research, 64,* 55–117.

Graham, S., Taylor, A. Z., & Hudley, C. (1998). Exploring achievement values among ethnic minority early adolescents. *Journal of Educational Psychology, 90,* 606–620.

Harter, S. (1988). *The self-perception profile for adolescents.* Unpublished manual, University of Denver, Colorado.

Harter, S. (1998). The development of self-representations. In W. Damon (Series Ed.) & N. Eisenberg (Vol. Ed.), *Handbook of child psychology: Vol. 3. Social, emotional, and personality development* (5th ed., pp. 553–617). New York: Wiley.

Harter, S. (1999). *Developmental approaches to self-processes.* New York: Guilford Press.

Harter, S., & Robinson, N. (1988). *The Social Support Scale for Older Children and Adolescents (Revised): Approval, emotional, and instrumental support.* Unpublished manual, University of Denver, Denver, Colorado.

Hudley, C., & Graham, S. (2001). Stereotypes of achievement striving among early adolescents. *Social Psychology of Education, 5,* 201–224.

Juvonen, J., & Wentzel, K. R. (Eds.). (1996). *Social motivation: Understanding children's school adjustment.* New York: Cambridge University Press.

Kenny, D. A., & DePaulo, B. M. (1993). Do people know how others view them? An empirical and theoretical account. *Psychological Bulletin, 114,* 145–161.

Kline, R. B. (1998). *Principles and practice of structural equation modeling.* New York: Guilford Press.

Linn, M. C., & Hsi, S. (2000). *Computers, teachers, peers: Science learning partners.* Mahwah, NJ: Erlbaum.

Ma, X. (2001). Participation in advanced mathematics: Do expectation and influence of students, peers, teachers, and parents matter? *Contemporary Educational Psychology, 26,* 132–146.

Madon, S., Smith, A., Jussim, L., Russell, D. W., Eccles, J. S., Palumbo, P., & Walkiewica, M. (2001). Am I as you see me or do you see me as I am? Self-fulfilling prophecies and self-verification. *Personality and Social Psychology Bulletin, 27,* 1214–1224.

Marsh, H. W. (1990). The causal ordering of academic self-concept and academic achievement: A multiwave, longitudinal panel analysis. *Journal of Educational Psychology, 82,* 646–656.

McLoyd, V. C. (1998). Changing demographics in the American population: Implications for research on minority children and adolescents. In V. C. McLoyd & L. Steinberg (Eds.), *Studying minority adolescents: Conceptual, methodological, and theoretical issues* (pp. 3–28). Mahwah, NJ: Erlbaum.

Mead, G. H. (1934). *Mind, self, and society from the standpoint of a social behaviorist.* Chicago: University of Chicago Press.

Meece, J. L., Parsons, J. E., Kaczala, C. M., Goff, S. B., & Futterman, R. (1982). Sex differences in math achievement: Toward a model of academic choice. *Psychological Bulletin, 91,* 324–348.

Miller, S., & Davis, T. L. (1992). Beliefs about children: A comparative study of mothers, teachers, peers, and self. *Child Development, 63,* 1251–1265.

National Commission on Mathematics and Science Teaching for the 21st Century. (2000). *Before it's too late.* Washington, DC: U.S. Department of Education.

Peng, S. S., Wright, D., & Hill, S. T. (1995). *Understanding racial-ethnic differences in secondary school science and mathematics achievement.* Washington, DC: U.S. Department of Education.

Phillips, D. A. (1987). Socialization of perceived academic competence among highly competent children. *Child Development, 58,* 1308–1320.

Pratt, M. W., Green, D., MacVicar, J., & Bountrogianni, M. (1992). The mathematical parent: Parental scaffolding, parent style, and learning outcomes in long-division mathematics homework. *Journal of Applied Developmental Psychology, 13,* 17–34.

Rosenthal, R. (2002). The Pygmalion effect and its mediating mechanisms. In J. Aronson (Ed.), *Improving academic achievement: Impact of psychological factors on education* (pp. 25–36). Orlando: Academic Press.

Rosenthal, R., & Jacobson, L. (1968). *Pygmalion in the classroom.* Austin, TX: Holt, Rinehart and Winston.

Steinberg, L. (1996). *Beyond the classroom: Why school reform has failed and what parents need to do.* New York: Simon & Schuster.

Wentzel, K. R. (1998). Social relationships and motivation in middle school: The role of parents, teachers, and peers. *Journal of Educational Psychology, 90,* 202–209.

Wentzel, K. R. (1999). Social-motivational processes and interpersonal relationships: Implications for understanding motivation at school. *Journal of Educational Psychology, 91,* 76–97.

Wigfield, A., & Eccles, J. S. (Eds.). (2002). *Development of achievement motivation.* San Diego: Academic Press.

Wigfield, A., & Harold, R. D. (1992). Teacher beliefs and children's achievement self-perceptions: A developmental perspective. In D. H. Schunk & J. L. Meece (Eds.), *Student perceptions in the classroom* (pp. 95–121). Mahwah, NJ: Erlbaum.

HEATHER A. BOUCHEY is assistant professor of psychology at the University of Vermont.

4

Narrative theories of personality help elucidate the complexity of success.

Science Success, Narrative Theories of Personality, and Race Self Complexity: Is Race Represented in the Identity Construction of African American Adolescents?

Cynthia E. Winston, David Wall Rice,
Brandi J. Bradshaw, Derek Lloyd, Lasana T. Harris,
Tanisha I. Burford, Gerard Clodimir, Karmen Kizzie,
Kristin Joy Carothers, Vetisha McClair, Jennifer Burrell

From what I have learned I mean there are African Americans that are pretty much proud of their race, and see themselves as somebody, and strong minded, intelligent, um hard working people.
—Malcolm

This research was supported in part by a grant to the first author from the National Science Foundation CAREER award (no. 0238485), by fellowship support to the first author while at Brown University from the Howard Hughes Medical Institute, and by grants to Jacquelynne S. Eccles and Arnold J. Sameroff from the MacArthur Network on Successful Adolescent Development in High-Risk Settings and the National Institutes for Child Health and Human Development. The authors would like to thank the following individuals for their comments on earlier drafts of this chapter: A. Wade Boykin, Jacquelynne Eccles, Kimberley Edelin Freeman, James Jones, Robert Sellers, Gina Paige, Judith Winston, Michael Winston, and James Wyche. Any opinions, findings, and conclusions or recommendations expressed in this material are those of the author(s) and do not necessarily reflect the views of the National Science Foundation.

Well when I was younger, I feel I didn't have to prove myself, but as I got older found that it. . . . that you have to. . . . kind of do have to prove yourself, so. More when I got older I found that out, but not when I was younger.
    —Karen

We have an attitude. . . . you're always, you just. . . . mad. You feel like you have to get back at everybody else for all the years of oppression and stuff like that. A lot of African Americans feel that because of what their ancestors went through with slavery, that this is supposed to, now that we're free, we're supposed to fight back. Not necessarily fight back physically, but fight back in, um, like to succeed. Do all the things that other, like white people told us we couldn't do, or never could do, stuff like that. I feel, it's not, it shouldn't be. I mean that was in the past.
    —LaToya

Prince George's County MADICS Study
High-achieving science and mathematics high school students

Given the critical role of science, mathematics, and technology in society, the success of all U.S. students in these areas is fundamental to their future success and quality of life, as well as to the economic well-being, standard of living, and national security of the United States. The current science and mathematics performance of African American students in the nation's schools raises considerable concern about their opportunities to participate fully in society in ways that allow them to have a high-quality standard of living and to make contributions to the advancement and well-being of the society. Among all U.S. elementary and secondary students, African American students have the lowest science performance in the nation on national assessments. According to the Nation's Report Card from the 2000 National Assessment of Educational Progress, only 7 percent of African American eighth graders and 3 percent of African American twelfth graders are proficient in mathematics (National Center for Educational Statistics, 2002). The low mathematics performance of African American students has persisted for more than a decade (see Figure 4.1).

The trend of low performance in science and mathematics among African American students in elementary and secondary education is not surprising, given the failure of the nation's schools to reach full excellence and equity in educating all its students. It is well established that African Americans have fewer opportunities than other students to learn science and mathematics. Compared to their White counterparts, African American students in the nation's schools experience less extensive and less demanding science and mathematics curricula and programs; low expectations and judgments of their ability that lead to tracking; fewer precollege programs; less qualified science teachers; less access to resources such as science facilities and equipment; and fewer opportunities within the classroom to

Figure 4.1. Percentage of Black and White 8th and 12th Grade Students Proficient in Mathematics

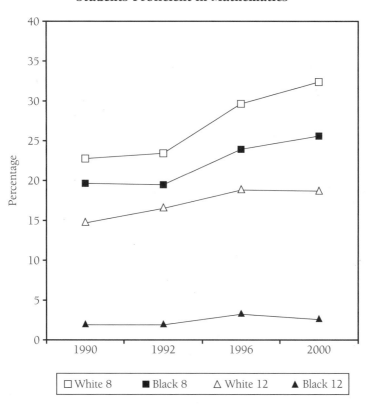

develop problem-solving and inquiry skills (Adelman, 1998; Anderson, Bruschie, & Pearson, 1994; Camara & Schimdt, 1999; Campbell, Denes, & Morrison, 2000; Clewell, Anderson, & Thorpe, 1992; Finn, 1999; Darling-Hammond, 1985, 1987; Maton, Hrabowski, & Schmitt, 2000; Oakes, 1987, 1990). In schools serving primarily students who are poor and have minority status, less than 50 percent of science and mathematics teachers are certified in the subject (National Commission on Mathematics and Science Teaching for the 21st Century, 2000).

Of all the self and social processes that could be examined in relation to science and mathematics achievement, identity is particularly important. It is well established that identity formation is a major developmental task of adolescence and one of the most important aspects of personality development. Moreover, for African American adolescents race has the potential to play a critical role in their identity formation. There is mounting empirical evidence that racial identity of African American students is related to their overall academic performance (Chavous et al., 2003; Grantham & Ford, 2003). However, there are inconsistencies about the nature of this relationship across studies (Arroyo & Zigler, 1995; Fordham & Ogbu, 1986; Lockett & Harrell, 2003). These inconsistencies may be explained through conducting research that focuses on an in-depth understanding of the identity of African American adolescents, including how race is represented in identity construction. Studying the identity of African American adolescents who have achieved success would allow researchers to understand the nature of identity of those who have demonstrated high academic achievement. One study that examined the identity construction of successful African American adolescent males revealed the complexities and function of identity construction and how it can serve as an integral dimension of adolescent males' motivation for success (Rice, 2004).

The focus of research to date that has examined the relationship between racial identity and academic achievement does not specifically focus on science and mathematics achievement. However, it is likely that racial identity is as important, if not more important, in achievement in these two subjects. Science and mathematics are subjects often perceived to be based on innate intellectual ability. Within U.S. society, there are pervasive intellectual stereotypes about African Americans' intellectual inferiority (Bobo & Kluegel, 1997; Jones, 1997; Steele & Aronson, 1995). How then do African American adolescents reconcile these negative stereotypes in the context of striving for success in science and mathematics?

In this chapter, we make three theoretical arguments regarding new directions for research on how identity is related to the science and mathematics achievement of African American adolescents. First, we contend that more research on science and mathematics achievement should focus on studying the identity construction of African American adolescents like Malcolm, Karen, and LaToya (see the quotations that opened the chapter), who are successful in these subjects. Second, we suggest that race is a *psychological* context for personality development and, therefore, must be considered in all analyses of the human development of African American adolescents. Third, we argue that narrative theories of personality have been underutilized in research on identity in general, as well as specifically within research on African American adolescents; yet they offer opportunities to answer important theoretical questions about the identity of African Americans who have succeeded in science and mathematics. In concluding this chapter, we recommend the development of a new theoretical framework that explains how race adds complexity to the self in ways that shape the identity construction of individuals who have achieved success in science and mathematics.

In this chapter, we adopt a distinctive approach to making these three theoretical arguments about the identity of African American adolescents who have achieved success in science and mathematics. Throughout the chapter, we will use the discourse of three adolescents who have high science and mathematics achievement to provide support for these theoretical arguments. The discourse of these adolescents will also be used to raise questions about new directions for research on the identity of African American adolescents who are succeeding in science and mathematics.

In articulating what this theoretical chapter will address, it is equally important to describe what will not be included. First, we will not provide an in-depth description of the research study that includes Malcolm, Karen, and LaToya (see Chavous et al., 2003, for study description). The use of their narratives and discourse is designed to provide support and illustrations for the theoretical arguments that are made and to raise questions for future research. Second, unlike the other chapters in this volume, we will not explicitly identify variables that predict science achievement of African American adolescents. Rather, our ultimate goal is to argue that the way race is represented in African American adolescents' identity construction is theoretically important in understanding their success in science and mathematics. Finally, one argument made in this chapter is that race is a psychological context for personality development of African American adolescents. Critical to this argument is consideration of variation in how race is experienced, understood, and socialized across historical, generational, gender, and socioeconomic lines (Stewart, 2003). However, due to the scope of the arguments advanced and space limitations, there will not be a theoretical discussion of these variations.

Science Success and African American Adolescents: Why Should More Research Be Conducted on Adolescents Who Have Achieved Success in Science and Mathematics?

Although the current achievement status of African American students (as a population) in science and mathematics is alarming, there is some good news. Emerging empirical evidence from both national and regional data indicates that on average, African American adolescents are optimistic and have high expectations for their success in science and mathematics, believe that high science and mathematics performance is important for their future success, and believe they have the ability to perform well in science and mathematics (Winston & Eccles, 2001; Freeman & Winston, 2001; Winston, Eccles, Senior, & Vida, 1997).

We argue that given the inequity in educational opportunity, coupled with the fact that a small percentage of African American students are succeeding, researchers interested in science and mathematics achievement of African American students should study more often those who have achieved success in these subjects. Psychological research on the academic achievement of African American students is more likely to pursue questions oriented toward why students fail rather than how students succeed. Knowing why a student fails will not necessarily lead to direct answers about how he or she can succeed. Thus we argue that to increase the success of African Americans in science and mathematics we need to make a more concerted effort to understand the educational and psychological experiences of those who have achieved success.

There are at least two distinct approaches that can be adopted to study the aspects of identity related to the science and mathematics achievement of adolescents who have demonstrated successful performance in these subjects. In the first approach, a survey research design coupled with discriminant analysis can be used to identify the identity variables that discriminate between students who are successful in science and mathematics those who are not. In the second approach, record data of grades could be combined with a case study or narrative research design. Using this approach, the record data would be used to identify students who have high science and mathematics achievement. Then narrative and case study research designs could be coupled with discursive, content, thematic, or grounded theory analysis to understand the identity of these successful students.

It is our position that this latter approach can complement the first and should be considered more often by researchers interested in understanding identity related to African American adolescents' science and mathematics achievement. Moreover, as the rest of the chapter will illustrate, this latter approach is more likely than the first to advance theory development through capturing the complexities of how race is represented in the identity construction of African American adolescents who have succeeded in science and mathematics. In other words, case study and narrative research designs are by nature better suited than other strategies of inquiry and research methods for understanding complexity, episodes of nuances, the sequentiality of experiences in context, and the wholeness of individuals (Camic, Rhodes, & Yardley, 2003; Denzin & Lincoln, 2000; Stake, 1995; Yin, 2003).

Moving Beyond a Category: Can Race Serve as a Context for Personality Development?

How has race been conceptualized in developmental research on African American adolescents?

With the exception of research on racial and ethnic identity, the majority of published research in developmental psychology that includes African American adolescents largely conceptualizes race as a demographic category to which individuals belong. Although some researchers integrate analysis and interpretation of the experiences that are linked to this category, few directly investigate how race is represented in African Americans' identity or how this relates to other aspects of their psychological functioning. Several scholars have reviewed extensively the research on African American children and adolescents (see Boykin & Ellison, 1995; Graham, 1994; Lee, 2003; McLoyd, 1991; McLoyd & Randolph, 1984; McLoyd & Steinberg, 1998). These scholars have recommended that researchers integrate culture and ecological considerations in the conceptual and interpretative frameworks.

However, these suggestions have been slow to be incorporated into oretical and methodological orientation of most of the published resea African American adolescents.

We contend that race, from a psychological perspective, should be conceptualized as a context for human development. The relationship between the individual and his or her environment has been the focus of psychological inquiry for some time. Within the last decade, there has been an increasing emphasis among developmental researchers that the incorporation of context is critical to a comprehensive understanding. Peers, families, neighborhood, and schools have been the primary developmental contexts emphasized. For African Americans, however, the nature of how race is experienced makes it something that should be considered as a dynamic context for development. Damon (1996) argues that developmental psychologists often conceptualize social context and its variation as a factor that has an external impact on individuals rather than as a dynamic set of practices in which the individual actively participates.

In this chapter, we hope to demonstrate that for researchers who have the goal of understanding the development of African American adolescents, neglecting race as a psychological context is short sighted, because it will lead to an incomplete understanding of how race is understood, experienced, and socialized. Consideration of race as a context of personality development will require clarity on the question, "What is race?"

Toward Two New Psychological Perspectives: What Is Race?

If race is a context for personality development for African American adolescents, researchers must articulate explicitly what they are referring to when using the term *race* in research. We have developed two new psychological perspectives of race that we contend are useful for research on African Americans. Although some dimensions of these perspectives may have applicability to other social and cultural groups, we have developed them in the context of the unique historical, social, and political experiences of African Americans in the United States. We acknowledge that the inherent complexities and difficulties of the issue of race in society make it impossible to create absolute conceptually definitive perspectives of race. We believe, however, that the two psychological perspectives of race we offer are useful. It is important to acknowledge that these two perspectives of race are developed in the context of full recognition that scientific evidence confirms that there are no biological races (Long & Kittles, 2003).

The Biopsychological Perspective of Race. We argue that from a biopsychological perspective, race has meaning for African Americans in terms of phenotypic variation and visibility. A biological process occurs in which melanasomes inside cells, called the malanocytes, produce melanin in the skin. This in turn produces a wide spectrum of skin color among human beings, with individuals of African descent having the largest range of skin tone variation among human populations. In many social contexts within the United States that are not predominantly Black, an individual's brown skin can create a certain type of visibility that has the potential to shape the attitudes and behavior of other people. In other social contexts that are predominantly Black, skin tone variation among African Americans also can shape others' attitudes and behaviors (Bradshaw, 2004; McClair, 2003). Therefore, for most African Americans phenotypic visibility and variation provide a link between biology and their psychological functioning. This link requires African Americans to make sense of the meaning they themselves as well as others attach to skin color visibility and variation.

Stereotype activation and stereotype application are psychological processes that provide an example of how the biopsychological perspective of race is relevant to the identity of African American high-achieving science and mathematics students. Within social psychological research, stereotype activation is the extent to which a stereotype is accessible in one's mind; stereotype application is the extent to which one uses a stereotype to judge a member of a stereotyped group (Kunda & Spencer, 2003). In interpersonal situations or interactions between students and teachers, stereotypes of African Americans can be elicited with a skin color cue or stimulus that signals that a person is an African American. An example of a pervasive stereotype in society is the intellectual inferiority of African Americans (Bobo & Kluegel, 1997). In a science or mathematics classroom, this is one stereotype that could be elicited by a teacher or other students. The basis of this stereotype activation could be largely based on categorization based on the skin color of the student. Category accessibility is a state of perceptual readiness that makes the category available for use in judgments such as identification, categorization, and inference about category members (Kunda & Spencer, 2003). If stereotype activation occurs, it could influence a teacher's expectations of what that student could achieve, which is a well-established pattern in science and mathematics classrooms (Oakes, 1987, 1990). Another possibility is that the societal stereotype that African Americans do not work hard (Bobo & Kluegel, 1997) could be elicited in the context of a science or mathematics classroom. This could lead to stereotyped judgments about the amount of effort a student will expend on studying science and mathematics.

Within a science or mathematics classroom, how can a teacher's stereotype activation shape how an African American student constructs his or her identity? There is evidence that teachers can communicate their low expectations of students through their behaviors as well as nonverbal expression (Jussim & Eccles, 1995). If an African American student perceives that a stereotype about his or her intellectual ability or work ethic is activated and applied, he or she can either accept that stereotype as defining his or her intellectual ability or work ethic, or can reject that stereotype as a self-definition. In either case, it is possible that the student's achievement motivation in science and mathematics would be undermined. Another possibility is that this perception of a stereotype could facilitate success by serving as a challenge that the student decides to take on to "prove" herself or himself in much the same way Karen describes. There is preliminary evidence that for some African American students in certain learning contexts, stereotype activation promotes mathematics performance (Harris, 2003) rather than undermines performance as with stereotype threat (Steele & Aronson, 1995). Considerably more research is needed to unravel these patterns of relations between teachers' stereotype activation based on skin color cues; students' perception of the stereotype activation; and students' identity construction, achievement motivation, and performance. Given that the majority of research in social psychology on stereotypes focuses on those who hold stereotypes rather than on the "target" of the stereotype, little is known about how and when African Americans perceive that someone has either activated a stereotype, applied a stereotype, or both (Shelton, 2000).

We contend that science and mathematics are important subjects for more in-depth examination of these patterns. One reason is that there is already evidence that low expectations of African American students are pervasive in science and mathematics classrooms. Yet there may be some students for whom these low expectations do not undermine their achievement motivation and performance. Can this be explained by how they construct their identity within these classrooms? The continued practice of tracking in U.S. public education also make science and mathematics important subjects in which to examine these patterns of relations. Within large integrated middle schools and high schools, African American students who are high achievers in science and mathematics are often tracked. As a result, they frequently find themselves in science and mathematics classrooms in which they experience racial isolation. Racial isolation in classrooms where success in these subjects is all too often perceived by the teacher and learner to be based on innate ability could cause adolescents to struggle with constructing an identity that will facilitate their achievement motivation and success. Adopting a biopsychological perspective of race acknowledges that skin color is a visible physical characteristic that is based on a biological process, which in turn requires African Americans to make sense of the meaning they themselves, as well as others, attach to what it means to be Black in U.S. society.

The Cultural Historical Perspective of Race. The cultural historical perspective of race recognizes that human development is a cultural process that occurs within the context of structured socioeconomic, political, and legal relations across time. In the United States, such relations have developed over time in distinctive ways because of the prominent role that race has played in the stratification of social groups and economic behavior (Jaynes & Williams, 1989). In the first two centuries of the country's history, this was largely attributable to the use of slave labor and to the fact that slaves were racially identifiable. After the abolition of slavery, race and racial classifications became even more important in the political and social system of the United States because of the rise of the white supremacy ideology (Jaynes & Williams, 1989). This doctrine structured society in such a way that with few exceptions, African Americans were in the lowest strata of the racial hierarchy and Whites were in the highest. This system was institutionalized by the adoption of statutory segregation in the South and its acceptance by the Supreme Court of the United States and the Congress. These social structures, born out of segregation by law and custom, created the disparities in income, housing, education, and other aspects of daily living that became for at least a century the social context of cultural development for African Americans.

This system of racial stratification in the United States has created differences in the life experiences of African Americans, compared to Whites and other groups with minority status. African Americans tend to reside in communities that have higher jobless rates and lower employment growth, as well as reduced access to employment (Wilson, 1987). The unemployment rate of Black men is three times the rate for White men (DeBarros & Bennett, 1997). For those who are employed, Black men earn seventy-eight cents for each dollar earned by their White counterparts (U.S. Bureau of Labor Statistics, 1997). As a result, the median income for Black families is only 55 percent of the median income for White families (Conley, 1999). When comparing White and African American families of the same income, White families have a significant advantage in terms of wealth, such that at the upper income levels, White families have a median net worth almost three times that of upper-income African American families. At the lower income levels, African American families have no assets, whereas the White family of the same income has $10,000 worth of equity (Survey Research Center, 1994).

Over time, these life experiences and their associated adaptive responses, coupled with retentions of African culture, have created a unique cultural context in which African American adolescents develop. Jones (2003) defines culture as psychological, symbolic, historical, and dynamic. The cultural historical perspective of race recognizes that development is a cultural process and that the unique historical and contemporary experiences of African Americans give race psychological meaning that is incorporated into cultured patterns of thought, feelings, and actions. The unique historical experiences of African Americans demand that African Americans develop a conception of who they are within a cultural historical frame of reference. This conception of race is similar to aspects of Vygotsky's sociocultural theory (1978), which posits that an individual's development must be understood within its social and cultural historical context and cannot be separated from it. This perspective of race does not equate culture and race. Rather, it assumes that the psychological significance of race evolves over time within cultural communities such that ways of thinking about race can eventually become part of a culture.

Jones (2003) describes a universal context of racism as one dimension of the cultural context in which African Americans develop; African Americans live daily with the possibility of threat, bias, denigration, denial, and truncated opportunities. Racism is a psychological reality at any given time for targets, and it that reality consists of the target's personal, as well as collective, racial pasts and futures, and their construal of the racial nature of their immediate experience. There are two types of motivational consequences that are triggered by the universal context of racism: self-protective motivations and self-enhancing motivations. Both of these motivational tendencies are triggered by the universal context of racism (Jones, 2003, p. 220).

LaToya's construction of her identity, as reflected in the following passage, represents one way in which a cultural historical conceptualization of race may be useful in research on the identity of African American adolescents who have achieved success in science and mathematics.

> We have an attitude. . . . you're always, you just. . . . mad. You feel like you have to get back at everybody else for all the years of oppression and stuff like that. A lot of African Americans feel that because of what their ancestors went through with slavery, that this is supposed to, now that we're free, we're supposed to fight back. Not necessarily fight back physically, but fight back in, um, like to succeed. Do all the things that other, like white people told us we couldn't do, or never could do, stuff like that. I feel, it's not, it shouldn't be. I mean that was in the past.

LaToya seems to construct an understanding of herself and success that is linked to the unique historical experience of African Americans in terms of what they "went through with slavery." Thus, even though slavery was a legal institution more than a hundred years ago and was not something that LaToya experienced directly, it is represented in her construction of both herself and African Americans. It is also linked to her motives for success. Initially she selects language to describe a collective *we*, then moves to an individual *you are* ("you're"). Then she makes a decision to use what could be considered a qualifier, "a lot of African Americans." Does understanding LaToya's motives for her success require serious consideration of her conception of who she is within a cultural historical frame of reference?

In sum, we have argued that race from a psychological perspective is a context for personality development of African American adolescents and that any consideration of race within research requires a clear rationale for how it is conceptualized and defined within the context of research. Toward this end, we propose a conceptualization of race that can serve to guide thinking about human development of African Americans. Although the two psychological perspectives of race that we have developed to guide research are not exhaustive, they are important to advancing the arguments made in this chapter. These perspectives can move research beyond conceptualizing race in terms of a category to which an individual belongs and can provide new directions in informing the types of research questions that are posed in research on the identity of African American adolescents who achieve success in science and mathematics.

Narrative Theories of Personality

What is the utility of narrative theories of personality in research on identity? Narrative has long been of interest to scholars interested in personality. McAdams (1999) asserts that narrative assumptions are explicit within some of the field's most well known "grand theories" of personality, including those of Adler (1927), Jung (1969), Murray (1938), and Erikson (1950). He characterizes all these theories as expressing "considerable interest in the temporal nature of human lives, how lives develop over time and how human beings understand that development" (p. 483). Although researchers often think of narrative as a research method or product of data collection, narrative can also be conceptualized as a psychosocial construction coauthored by the individual and the cultural context in which that person's life is embedded and given meaning (McAdams, 2001). As such, narrative integrates the cognitive, affective, and motivation systems of personality and is a part of personality and psychological functioning (Singer, 1995).

Narrative theories of personality emphasize that as humans develop they create internalized narratives and stories. There is a diversity of overlapping narrative theories of personality. Some of the more widely studied narrative theories of personality include the following: identity as a life story (McAdams, 1985); script theory (Tomkins, 1979); the dialogical self (Hermans, 1988); and self-defining narrative memory (Singer, 1995).

Several researchers have adopted narrative theories of personality in research on the identity of adolescents (Habermas & Bluck, 2000; McKeough & Genereux, 2003); however, these theories have been largely underutilized to date. Yet narrative theories of personality have utility for understanding three psychological issues related to identity that are important for understanding individuality, one of the goals of personality psychology. These three psychological issues are identity construction, function, and complexity. We will discuss how narrative theories of personality are valuable theoretical guides for understanding each of these, particularly during the period of adolescence.

Narrative theories of personality have utility for guiding conceptualization of identity as a construction. This construction reflects individuality and is performed by an individual. Advances in cognitive development enable adolescents to engage in formal operational thinking, which psychologically positions them not just for possessing or having an identity but also for creating identity. Narrative theories of personality have utility for understanding identity because they focus on the way individuals configure or shape the self. Internalized stories of self serve to bring into focus the recollected past, perceived present, and anticipated future. Thus the narrative constructed is a selective, interpretive representation of self.

Narrative theories of personality place the individual on center stage with interpretive power as an author of identity. From this perspective, questions arise about the psychological function narrative serves for the person. In general, narrative theories of personality assert that the creation of an internalized narrative of self is motivated by a need for psychological unity and purpose (McAdams, 1999, 2001; Singer, 1995). Adolescence is arguably one of the most theoretically interesting times in the life course in which to pose questions about identity construction and the function of identity, yet it is also one of the most psychologically complex. Adolescence serves as a biological, psychological, and social bridge between childhood and adulthood. It involves simultaneous biological, cognitive, social, and emotional changes.

Considerable development and experience have occurred before the individual reaches adolescence. Therefore, these changes converge with an already well-developed personality. As a result, identity is very complicated and complex for adolescents, who often experience a struggle between their psychological individuality and their similarity with others. Narrative theories of personality, with their focus on questions about the hows and whys of construction and function, inherently take on the challenge of complexity as essential for full understanding of identity and the systems of personality.

Habermas and Bluck (2000) argue that the prerequisite cognitive tools for constructing global coherence in a narrative, as well as the social and motivational demands to construct a narrative, develop during adolescence. They suggest that this psychological readiness for creation of an internalized narrative converges with societal and adult pressures for adolescents to "get a life." Therefore, adolescence is in a sense the infancy of the narrative, making it an ideal developmental period for the study of identity of individuals who have achieved success.

What is the utility of narrative theories of personality for research on the identity construction of African American adolescents who have achieved success in science and mathematics?

From a biopsychological and cultural historical perspective of race, the identity construction of African Americans who have achieved success in science and mathematics is particularly complex. Because of this complexity, narrative theories of personality provide a valuable theoretical tool for further understanding, not only because of their focus on identity construction, function, and complexity but also because they recognize that "narratives are intelligible within a particular cultural frame, and yet they differentiate one person from the next" (McAdams, 2001, p. 101). Narrative theories are thus valuable guides to understanding and examining how race, from a biopsychological and cultural historical perspective, is represented in an individual's internalized narrative of self, something not easily accessible because of its complexity.

Self-defining memory, for example, is one narrative theory of personality that provides a useful theoretical framework for developing new understanding of the identity of African American adolescents who have achieved success in science and mathematics. This theory seeks to explain how an individual confronts the challenge of evaluating, categorizing, and ordering all the competing demands of internal and external stimuli such that he or she "fixes" a perception into consciousness (Singer, 1995; Singer & Salovey, 1993). In constructing an understanding of self, how does Malcolm attend to the internal stimuli of understanding a group of which he is a member as "strong minded, intelligent, um hard working people" (see chapter-opening quotation), while simultaneously encountering competing and pervasive external stimuli of persistent racial stereotypes of his group as weak minded, dumb, and lazy (Bobo & Kluegel, 1997)?

Does Malcolm's construction of group-defining traits that are directly opposite those most often associated with his group in society serve a particular adaptive function? Are Malcolm's evaluation and categorization of the external stimuli of racial intellectual stereotypes of African Americans serving not only as a mechanism for him to define himself in the opposite way but also as a motive for his own academic success? Are intellectual stereotypes of African Americans a pronounced and meaningful part of the external stimuli that Malcolm integrates into the construction of his identity?

An individual relies on narrative as a perceptual aid or means of internal sight (Singer, 1995). This internal sight is not just automatic, but is the emergent product of what Singer describes as three hierarchical principles of the I-Self, as well as action on the part of the Me-Self. Singer suggests that the self as subject or knower (I-Self) employs three hierarchical principles of organization—evaluation, categorization, and subsidiation—that facilitate greater and greater distinctions in the I-Self's world of internal and external demands. According to Singer, these principles guide the development of the cognitive, affective, motivational, behavioral, and psychophysiological systems of personality. In turn, the interaction of these systems creates multiple Me-Selves that are composed of the different roles and contexts of the personality. Within each of these Me-Selves are evaluations (valenced responses to self and others), categories (self- and other representations) and sequences in time (the self and others in the past, present, and future). In the context of discussing her academic achievement and success, Karen, for example, defines herself as an active agent in demonstrating having to "prove" her ability to others in ways that were not required of her when she was younger. In constructing her identity, she uses sequences in developmental time that are repeated in the same pattern.

"Well when I was younger, I feel I didn't have to prove myself, but as I got older found that it. . . . that you have to. . . . kind of do have to prove yourself, so. More when I got older I found that out, but not when I was younger."

Does this repetitive developmental sequence of time and "proof" serve an adaptive function in Karen's internalized narrative of self? What is the nature of the external and internal stimuli that Karen is evaluating and categorizing in her integrative narrative of what she "found" about having to demonstrate a particular quality or worth or ability in order to "prove" herself?

Like Karen's segment of identity construction represented here, LaToya's raises many theoretical questions about the interplay of race, cognition, emotion, and motives for success that are further complicated by a different type of developmental and temporal sequence. In LaToya's identity construction, what is the psychological meaning of her decision to use the language of emotion? Is there a psychic tax or is ego depletion (Baumeister, Bratslavsky, Muraven, & Tice, 1998) occurring as LaToya tells the researcher about her emotions of having an "attitude. . . . always [being] mad" and feeling "like you always have to get back at everybody else for all the years of oppression and stuff like that"? Is there an interplay among LaToya's race-related emotion, achievement motives, and understanding of why success is important to her as an African American? Is it possible that racism or "all of the years of oppression and stuff like that" and what her "ancestors went through with slavery" serve as one, of many, motives for her success in science and mathematics? Could understanding the psychological function of this racism help us better understand the type of motives LaToya has for high science and mathematics achievement? Does LaToya's disposition with respect to racism of the past serve the psychological function of facilitating a belief in her abilities to succeed without ego depletion? In situations and contexts in which she perceives racism, does an understanding of race from a cultural historical perspective actually increase her capacity or willingness to engage in achievement-related behavior?

Race Self Complexity and New Directions for Research on Science Success

In our opinion, Malcolm, Karen, and LaToya reveal in fewer than thirteen sentences the complexity of race in the identity construction of African American adolescents who have achieved success in science and mathematics. What theoretical frameworks exist to explain that for some adolescents, creating an internalized story of self is bound by competing internal and external stimuli, some of which (but not certainly not all) are related to the psychological significance of race? We believe that narrative theories of personality provide a theoretical guide for the development of such a framework. These sentences also illustrate that understanding the self and social processes related to the science achievement of at least these three students would be distorted without a theoretical framework that explains how race, from a biopsychological and cultural historical perspective, is represented in their self system and identity construction.

Although there are many theorists who have contributed understanding to this psychological issue, there has not been an explicit personality theoretical framework developed to guide research on how race is represented in the self system of African Americans at its most complex level and that focuses on individuality, function, and complexity. We believe that such a theoretical framework of race self complexity needs to be developed. We recommend that one new direction for research on the identity of successful African American adolescents is to conduct research to understand systematically how race, from a biopsychological and cultural historical perspective, adds another layer of complexity to the self system and psychologically complicates identity construction.

Such a theoretical framework of race self complexity can be developed through careful, strategic, and complex research design. Emerging from this type of focused research design would be numerous studies conducted specifically to build a theory of race self complexity. In this beginning articulation of race self complexity, we contend that a theory of race self complexity would explain how race, from a biopsychological and cultural historical perspective, is represented within the self system of African Americans and adds complexity to this system. It also would explain how the self system, because of its well-established intricate structure, dynamics, motives, and functions, also creates complexity as to how race is understood, experienced, and socialized by African Americans. This two-way complexity is important to capture in a theory because it has implications for the socialization and personality development of African Americans who live in a society in which the psychological meaning of race at the institutional, individual, and cultural levels requires various patterns of adaptation. For the reasons we have articulated in this chapter, we contend that studying the lives of African Americans who are successful, especially in subjects that are thought to be based on innate ability, would be particularly useful for developing a theory of race self complexity. Race self complexity is proposed as a way to theoretically integrate research on the self (for example, Baumeister et al., 1998; Beach & Tesser, 1995; Krueger, 1998; Robins, Norem & Cheek, 1999) and research on the psychological significance of race (for example, Bowman & Howard, 1985; Boykin & Ellison, 1995; Cross, 1991; Cunningham & Spencer, 2000; Franklin & Boyd-Franklin, 2000; Harrell, 1999; Sellers, Rowley, Chavous, Shelton, & Smith, 1997; Stevenson, 2002; Way, 1998) to capture critical issues of individuality, complexity, and psychological function.

In summary, it is clear from the arguments in this chapter that there are many theoretical issues and questions that require further systematic inquiry to understand how race is represented in the identity construction of successful African American adolescents. As African American high achievers in science construct their academic identity, what is the interplay of cognitive, social, and emotional representations of race? In subjects such as science and mathematics, where success is perceived by many adolescents to be based on innate ability, are intellectual stereotypes of African Americans a pronounced and meaningful part of the academic identity African American adolescents construct? Does this always have to be a psychological liability, or are there situations in which intellectual stereotypes are part of their motives for academic success?

Conclusion

The purpose of this chapter was to make several theoretical arguments about new directions for research on the identity of African American adolescents who have succeeded in science and mathematics. We have argued that the way that race is represented in African American adolescents' identity construction is theoretically important in understanding their success in science and mathematics. We suggested that race from a biopsychological and cultural historical perspective is a *psychological* context for personality development. Therefore, race should be included in analyses of the human development of African American adolescents. In addition, we argued that narrative theories of personality offer opportunities to answer important theoretical questions about how race, from a biopsychological and cultural historical perspective, is represented in the identity construction of African American adolescents who have achieved success in science. We have approached the question of what new directions are necessary for research on the science and mathematics achievement of African Americans by using the discourse of three adolescents who are high achievers in science to posit a set of theoretical arguments about the complexity of identity of African American adolescents.

We believe that there is a need for scholars of human development to move the study of the identity of African American adolescents from an isolated context—where research on African American adolescents is thought of as contributing to the field knowledge exclusively about African Americans—to an integral context. African American adolescents are human, and therefore some of the discoveries about their identity and success have the potential to contribute to increasing understanding of human development. For example, research on African American adolescents can raise questions about knowledge of human development that has been developed created largely from research with white middle-class participants (Graham, 1994; McLoyd, 1991). In other words, if we are able to develop a theoretical framework to explain how race adds another layer of complexity to the self system of African Americans, it is likely that advances in understanding the function and motives of the self for all humans will be made as well.

In conclusion, it is important to consider the significance of the historical moment in which this chapter is written. Three related Supreme Court cases about race and educational equity have significance in defining the historical moment and the importance of how race is considered in research on science success. In spring 2003, the Supreme Court heard two cases challenging the constitutionality of the use of race in education, *Gratz v. University of Michigan* (2003) and *Grutter v. University of Michigan* (2003). The court determined that race can be used in educational decision making without offending the Constitution. These decisions suggest that the court recognizes that there continue to be unequal educational opportunities to learn. In other words, the premise of these decisions was that this racial inequity persists in the nation's public education system and should be considered when judging the high school achievement and performance of non-White students for university admission. At the same historical moment, national organizations and institutions throughout the country are celebrating the fifty-year anniversary of the historic Supreme Court case *Brown v. Board of Education* (1954), a case that has been described as the most significant Supreme Court decision about equal educational opportunity in the history of American jurisprudence (Winston, 2003).

Although African Americans have made considerable progress in educational opportunities and attainment in the fifty years since *Brown v. Board of Education* (Nettles, Perna, & Freeman, 1999), the nation has failed to reach *full* excellence and equity in educating all its citizens. This inequity is no more apparent than in science and mathematics. Moreover, this inequity in educational opportunity is occurring at a time when the report by the American Association for the Advancement of Science, *Science for All Americans* (1989, p. 1), asserts the following: "What the future holds in store for individual human beings, the nation and the world largely depends on the wisdom with which humans use science, math, and technology. And that, in turn depends on the character, distribution, and effectiveness of the education that people receive."

This is a historical moment in which psychologists have a critical role to play in research on the self and social processes related to the success of African American adolescents in science. We believe that the research of personality psychologists is critical because of our focus on understanding the person. The new directions proposed for research on the identity of African American adolescents who are high science achievers represent a recycling of history of sorts. In *Brown v. Board of Education* (1954), the psychological research of Kenneth Clark on identity and success of African Americans was integral to the argument advanced in this case that African American students' self-interpretations based on race were negative and self-hating and shaped their educational success. The Supreme Court's decision stated that "a sense of inferiority affects the motivation of a child to learn." Fifty years later, we too suggest that the self processes related to race, from a cultural historical and biopsychological perspective, are important for understanding success of African American students in science and therefore cannot be neglected in research on their academic development. We also contend that how race is represented in the self system of African American students is much more complex than the social science research could have reflected in

1954 because of the limited theoretical and methodological knowledge about race in social science at that time.

As only a few phrases constructed by three adolescents, Malcolm, Karen, and LaToya, reveal, race may be a psychological context for personality development and therefore for understanding success in science. Although understanding this piece of the identity puzzle will not magically create widespread success in science, it will add one of the more vital pieces that has been largely ignored in psychological research, as well as in discourse on national policy, program, and practice. Malcolm's, Karen's, and LaToya's words challenge all researchers who are invested in the future of the nation. Those interested in the success of all students will need to consider race self complexity as an important new direction for research. If it is our hope that fifty years from now, scholars of human development will be able to write the story of the science success of African American adolescents as a population, we cannot afford to silence the profound internal voices of society's Malcolms, Karens, and LaToyas.

References

Adelman, C. (1998). *Women and men of the engineering path: A model for analyses of undergraduate careers*. Washington, DC: U.S. Department of Education and the National Institute for Science Education.

Adler, A. (1927). *Understanding human nature*. Oxford: Greenberg.

American Association for the Advancement of Science. (1989). *Science for all Americans: Project 2061*. Washington, DC: American Association for the Advancement of Science.

Anderson, B. T., Bruschie, B. A., & Pearson, W. (1994). Minority females and precollege mathematics and science: Academic preparation and career interests. *Equity and Excellence in Education, 27*, 62–70.

Arroyo, C., & Zigler, E. (1995). Racial identity, academic achievement, and the psychological well-being of economically disadvantaged adolescents. *Journal of Personality and Social Psychology, 69*, 903–914.

Baumeister, R. F., Bratslavsky, E., Muraven, M., & Tice, D. M. (1998). Ego depletion: Is the active self a limited resource? *Journal of Personality and Social Psychology, 74*, 1252–1265.

Beach, S. R., & Tesser, A. (1995). Self-esteem and the extended self-evaluation maintenance model: The self in social context. In M. H. Kernis (Ed.), *Efficacy, agency, and self-esteem* (pp. 145–170). New York: Plenum.

Bobo, L., & Kluegel, J. R. (1997). Status, ideology and dimensions of whites' racial beliefs and attitudes: Progress and stagnation. In S. A. Tuch & J. K. Martin (Eds.), *Racial attitudes in the 1990s* (pp. 93–120). New York: Praeger.

Bowman, P. J., & Howard, C. (1985). Race-related socialization, motivation, and academic achievement: A study of black youths in three-generation families. *Journal of the American Academy of Child Psychiatry, 24*, 131–141.

Boykin, A. W., & Ellison, C. M. (1995). The multiple ecologies of black youth socialization: An afrographic analysis. In R. T. Taylor (Ed.), *African-American youth: Their social and economic status in the United States* (pp. 93–128). Westport, CT: Greenwood Press.

Bradshaw, B. J. (2004). *The color bar: Developing a research tool to examine the psychological significance of phenotypic variation and race self complexity*. Unpublished master's thesis, Howard University, Washington, DC.

Brown v. Board of Educ., 347 U.S. 483 (1954).

Camara, W. J., & Schimdt, A. E. (1999). *Group differences in standardized testing and social stratification.* New York: College Board.

Camic, P. M., Rhodes, J. E., & Yardley, L. (2003). Naming the stars: Integrating qualitative methods into psychological research. In P. Camic & J. Rhodes (Eds.), *Qualitative research in psychology: Expanding perspectives in methodology and design* (pp. 3–15). Washington, DC: American Psychological Association.

Campbell, G., Denes, R., & Morrison, C. (Eds.). (2000). *Access denied: Race, ethnicity, and the scientific enterprise.* New York: Oxford University Press.

Chavous, T. M., Bernat, D. H., Schmeelk, C. K., Caldwell, C. H., Kohn, L. W., & Zimmerman, M. A. (2003). Racial identity and academic attainment among African American adolescents. *Child Development, 74,* 1076–1090.

Clewell, B. C., Anderson, B. T., & Thorpe, M. E. (1992). *Breaking the barriers: Helping female and minority students succeed in mathematics and science.* San Francisco: Jossey-Bass.

Conley, D. (1999). *Being black, living in the red: Race, wealth, and social policy in America.* Berkeley: University of California Press.

Cross, W. E. (1991). *Shades of black: Diversity in African-American identity.* Philadelphia: Temple University Press.

Cunningham, M., & Spencer, M. B. (2000). Conceptual and methodological issues in studying minority adolescents. In R. Montemayor, G. R. Adams, & T. P. Gullotta (Eds.), *Adolescent diversity in ethnic, economic, and cultural contexts* (pp. 235–257). Thousand Oaks, CA: Sage.

Damon, W. (1996). Nature, second nature, and individual development: An ethnographic opportunity. In R. Jessor, A. Colby, & R. Shweder (Eds.), *Ethnography and human development: Context and meaning in social inquiry* (pp. 455–475). Chicago: University of Chicago Press.

Darling-Hammond, L. (1985). *Equality and excellence: The educational status of black Americans.* New York: College Board.

Darling-Hammond, L. (1987). Teacher quality and equality. In P. Keating & J. I. Goodland (Eds.), *Access to knowledge.* New York: College Board.

DeBarros, K., & Bennett, C. (1997). *The black population in the United States* (Current Population Reports, series P-20, No. 508). Washington, DC: U.S. Government Printing Office.

Denzin, N. K., & Lincoln, Y. S. (2000). The discipline and practice of qualitative research. In N. K. Denzin & Y. S. Lincoln (Eds.), *Handbook of qualitative research* (2nd ed., pp. 1–28). Thousand Oaks, CA: Sage.

Erikson, E. H. (1950). *Childhood and society.* New York: Norton.

Finn, J. D. (1999). Opportunity offered—opportunity taken: Course-taking in American high school. *ETS Policy Notes, 9,* 1–8.

Fordham, S., & Ogbu, J. (1986). Black students' school success: Coping with the "burden of acting white." *Urban Review, 18,* 176–206.

Franklin, A. J., & Boyd-Franklin, N. (2000). Invisibility syndrome: A clinical model of the effects of racism on African American males. *American Journal of Orthopsychiatry, 70*(1), 33–41.

Freeman, K. E., & Winston, C. E. (2001, April). *The relationship between race and the math performance of high school students: The relative contribution of student background and motivation.* Paper presented at the meeting of the American Educational Research Association, Seattle, WA.

Graham, S. (1994). Motivation in African Americans. *Review of Educational Research, 64,* 55–117.

Grantham, T., & Ford, D. (2003). Beyond self-concept and self-esteem: Racial identity and gifted African American students. *High School Journal, 87,* 18–29.

Gratz v. University of Michigan/Bollinger, 539 U.S. 244 (2003).

Grutter v. University of Michigan/Bollinger 539 U.S. 306 (2003).

Habermas, T., & Bluck, S. (2000). Getting a life: The emergence of the life story in adolescence. *Psychological Bulletin, 126,* 748–769.

Harrell, C.J.P. (1999). *Manichean psychology: Racism and the minds of people of African descent.* Washington, DC: Howard University Press.

Harris, L. (2003). *Testing the theory: Cognitive buffers and stereotype threat effects in a black college environment.* Unpublished senior honor's thesis, Howard University, Washington, DC.

Hermans, H. J. (1988). On the integration of nomothetic and idiographic research methods in the study of personal meaning. *Journal of Personality, 56,* 785–812.

Jaynes, G. J., & Williams, R. M. (1989). *A common destiny: blacks and American society. National Research Council, Committee on the Status of Black Americans.* Washington, DC: National Academy of Press.

Jones, J. M. (1997). *Prejudice and racism* (2nd ed.). New York: McGraw-Hill.

Jones, J. M. (2003). TRIOS: A psychological theory of the African legacy in American culture. *Journal of Social Issues, 59,* 217–241.

Jung, H. Y. (1969). Confucianism and existentialism: Intersubjectivity as the way of man. *Philosophy and Phenomenological Research, 30,* 186–202.

Jussim, L. J., & Eccles, J. (1995). Are teacher expectations biased by students' gender, social class or ethnicity? In Y. T. Lee, L.J. Jussim, & C. R. McCauley (Eds.), *Stereotype accuracy: Toward appreciating group difference* (pp. 245–271). Washington, DC: American Psychological Association.

Krueger, J. (1998). Enhancement bias in the description of self and others. *Personality and Social Psychology Bulletin, 24,* 505–516.

Kunda, Z., & Spencer, S. J. (2003). When do stereotypes come to mind and when do they color judgment? A goal-based theoretical framework for stereotype activation and application. *Psychological Bulletin, 129,* 522–544.

Lee, C. D. (2003). Why we need to re-think race and ethnicity in educational research. *Educational Researcher, 32,* 3–5.

Lockett, C. T., & Harrell, J. P. (2003). Racial identity, self-esteem, and academic achievement: Too much interpretation, too little supporting data. *Journal of Black Psychology, 29,* 325–336.

Long, J. C., & Kittles, R. A. (2003). Human genetic diversity and the nonexistence of biological races. *Human Biology, 75,* 449–471.

Maton, K. I., Hrabowski, F. A., & Schmitt, C. L. (2000). African American college students excelling in the sciences: College and post college outcomes in the Meyerhoff Scholars Programs. *Journal of Research in Science Teaching, 37,* 629–654.

McAdams, D. P. (1985). *Power, intimacy, and the life story: Personological inquiries into identity.* New York: Guilford Press.

McAdams, D.P. (1999). Personal narratives and the life story. In L. A. Pervin & O. P. John (Eds.), *Handbook of personality theory and research* (2nd ed., pp. 478–500). New York: Guilford Press.

McAdams, D. P. (2001). The psychology of life stories. *Review of General Psychology, 5,* 100–122.

McClair, V. (2003). Developing a strategy of inquiry and research instruments for studying skin color satisfaction in psychological research: How can the lived experiences and race self complexity of African Americans be understood? *Howard University Ronald McNair Program Journal of Research, 8,* 52–55.

McKeough, A., & Genereux, R. (2003). Transformation in narrative thought during adolescence: The structure and content of story compositions. *Journal of Educational Psychology, 95,* 537–552.

McLoyd, V. (1991). What is the study of African American children the study of? The conduct, publication, and changing nature of research on African American children. In R. L. Jones (Ed.), *Black psychology* (3rd ed., pp. 419–440). Berkeley, CA: Cobb and Henry.

McLoyd, V., & Randolph, S. (1984). The conduct and publication of research on Afro-American children: A content analysis. *Human Development, 27,* 65–75.

McLoyd, V., & Steinberg, L. (1998). *Studying minority adolescents: Conceptual, methodological, and theoretical issues.* Mahwah, NJ: Erlbaum.

Murray, J. M. (1938). The conscience during adolescence. *Mental Hygiene, 22,* 400–408.

National Center for Educational Statistics. (2002). *The nation's report card: The National Assessment of Educational Progress.* Washington, DC: U.S. Department of Education.

National Commission on Mathematics and Science Teaching for the 21st Century. (2000). *Before it's too late.* Washington, DC: U.S. Department of Education.

Nettles, M. T., Perna, L. W., & Freeman, K. E. (1999). *Two decades of progress: African Americans moving forward in higher education.* Fairfax, VA: Frederick D. Patterson Research Institute of The College Fund/UNCF.

Oakes, J. (1987). Tracking in secondary schools: A contextual perspective. *Educational Psychologist, 22,* 129–154.

Oakes, J. (1990). *Multiplying inequalities: The effects of race, social class, and tracking on opportunities to learn mathematics and science* (No. R-3928-NSF). Santa Monica, CA: Rand.

Rice, D. W. (2004). *Race self complexity: How is the function of double-consciousness manifest in the self-construction of successful African American adolescent males?* Unpublished dissertation, Howard University, Washington, DC.

Robins, R. W., Norem, J. K. & Cheek, J.M. (1999). Naturalizing the self. In L. A. Pervin & O. P. John (Eds.), *Handbook of personality theory and research* (2nd. ed., pp. 443–477). New York: Guilford Press.

Sellers, R. M., Rowley, S. A., Chavous, T. M., Shelton, J. N., & Smith, M. A. (1997). Multidimensional inventory of black identity: A preliminary investigation of reliability and construct validity. *Journal of Personality and Social Psychology, 73,* 808–815.

Shelton, J. N. (2000). A reconceptualization of how we study issues of racial prejudice. *Personality and Social Psychology Review, 4,* 374–390.

Singer, J. A. (1995). Seeing one's self: Locating narrative memory in a framework of personality. *Journal of Personality, 63,* 429–457.

Singer, J. A., & Salovey, P. (1993). *The remembered self: Emotion and memory in personality.* New York: Free Press.

Stake, R. E. (1995). *The art of case study research.* Thousand Oaks, CA: Sage.

Steele, C. M., & Aronson, J. (1995). Stereotype threat and the intellectual test performance of African Americans. *Journal of Personality and Social Psychology, 69,* 797–811.

Stevenson, H. C. (2002). Wrestling with destiny: Cultural socialization of anger and healing for African American males. *Journal of Psychology and Christianity, 21,* 357–364.

Stewart, A. (2003). Gender, race, and generation in a Midwest high school: Using ethnographically informed methods in psychology. *Psychology of Women Quarterly, 27*(1), 1–11.

Survey Research Center, Institute for Social Research at the University of Michigan. (1994). *Panel Study of Income Dynamics (PSID).* Available from the PSID website, http://www.isr.umich.edu/src/psid.

Tomkins, S. S. (1979). Script theory. In H. E. Howe & R. A. Dienstbier (Eds.), *Nebraska symposium on motivation* (Vol. 26, pp. 201–236). Lincoln: University of Nebraska Press.

U.S. Bureau of Labor Statistics. (1997). *Labor force statistics from the current population survey.* Washington, DC: U.S. Government Printing Office.

Vygotsky, L. S. (1978). *Mind in society: The development of higher psychological processes.* Cambridge, MA: Harvard University Press.

Way, N. (1998). *Everyday courage: The lives and stories of urban teenagers.* New York: New York University Press.

Wilson, W. (1987). *The truly disadvantaged: The inner city, the underclass, and public policy.* Chicago: University of Chicago Press.

Winston, C. E., & Eccles, J. S. (2001, August). *Expectancy-value theory and self-enhancement: Examining comparative math expectations and mathematics performance of African American adolescents.* Paper presented at the meeting of the American Psychological Association, San Francisco.

Winston, C. E., Eccles, J. S., Senior, A. M., & Vida, M. (1997). The utility of an expectancy-value model and disidentification models for understanding ethnic group differences in academic performance and self-esteem. *Zeitschrift für Pädagogische Psychologie, 11*(3–4), 177–186.

Winston, J. (2003). Rural schools in America: Will no child be left behind? The elusive quest for educational opportunities. *Nebraska Law Review, 82,* 190–210.

Yin, R. K. (2003). *Case study research: Design and methods* (3rd ed.). Thousand Oaks, CA: Sage.

CYNTHIA E. WINSTON is assistant professor of psychology at Howard University and principal investigator of the Identity and Success Research Laboratory. Her research focuses on race self complexity and the psychological significance of race and racism in successful African Americans' internalized narratives of self.

DAVID WALL RICE is a postdoctoral fellow at the Institute for Urban and Minority Education at Teachers College, Columbia University.

BRANDI J. BRADSHAW is a graduate student in the Department of Psychology at Howard University.

DEREK LLOYD is the senior engineer in the Office of the Senior Vice President of Howard University.

LASANA T. HARRIS is a graduate student in the Department of Psychology at Princeton University.

TANISHA I. BURFORD is a graduate student in the Department of Psychology at Howard University.

GERARD CLODIMIR is a graduate student in the Department of Human Development and Psychology at Harvard University.

KARMEN KIZZIE is a graduate student in the Department of Psychology at the University of Michigan.

KRISTIN JOY CAROTHERS is a case manager for the Crossroads Program at the DePaul University Community Mental Health Center.

VETISHA MCCLAIR is a graduate student in the Department of Educational Psychology at University of Illinois at Urbana-Champaign.

JENNIFER BURRELL is a graduate student in the Justice, Law and Society Program at American University.

INDEX

79

Back Issue/Subscription Order Form

Copy or detach and send to:

Jossey-Bass, A Wiley Company, 989 Market Street, San Francisco CA 94103-1741

Call or fax toll-free: Phone 888-378-2537 6:30AM – 3PM PST; Fax 888-481-2665

Back Issues: Please send me the following issues at $29 each
(Important: please include series initials and issue number, such as CAD96.)

_____

_____

_____

$ _____   Total for single issues

$ _____   SHIPPING CHARGES: SURFACE   Domestic   Canadian
                                    First Item $5.00 $6.00
                                    Each Add'l Item $3.00 $1.50
                  For next-day and second-day delivery rates, call the number listed above.

Subscriptions: Please __start __renew my subscription to *New Directions for Child and Adolescent Development* for the year 2____ at the following rate:

U.S.	__Individual $90	__Institutional $205
Canada	__Individual $90	__Institutional $245
All Others	__Individual $114	__Institutional $279
U.S. Online Subscription		__Institutional $205
U.S. Print and Online Subscription		__Institutional $226

For more information about online subscriptions visit
www.interscience.wiley.com

$_____   Total single issues and subscriptions (Add appropriate sales tax for your state for single issue orders. No sales tax for U.S. subscriptions. Canadian residents, add GST for subscriptions and single issues.)

__Payment enclosed (U.S. check or money order only)
__VISA __MC __AmEx #_____ Exp. Date _____

Signature _____ Day Phone _____
__ Bill Me (U.S. institutional orders only. Purchase order required.)

Purchase order # _____
                 Federal Tax ID13559302   GST 89102 8052

Name _____

Address _____

_____

Phone _____ E-mail _____

For more information about Jossey-Bass, visit our Web site at www.josseybass.com

OTHER TITLES AVAILABLE IN THE
NEW DIRECTIONS FOR CHILD AND ADOLESCENT DEVELOPMENT SERIES
William Damon, Editor-in-Chief

NEW DIRECTIONS FOR CHILD AND ADOLESCENT DEVELOPMENT IS NOW AVAILABLE ONLINE AT WILEY INTERSCIENCE

What is Wiley InterScience?

Wiley InterScience is the dynamic online content service from John Wiley & Sons delivering the full text of over 300 leading scientific, technical, medical, and professional journals, plus major reference works, the acclaimed Current Protocols laboratory manuals, and even the full text of select Wiley print books online.

What are some special features of Wiley InterScience?

Wiley Interscience Alerts is a service that delivers table of contents via e-mail for any journal available on Wiley InterScience as soon as a new issue is published online.

EarlyView is Wiley's exclusive service presenting individual articles online as soon as they are ready, even before the release of the compiled print issue. These articles are complete, peer-reviewed, and citable.

CrossRef is the innovative multi-publisher reference linking system enabling readers to move seamlessly from a reference in a journal article to the cited publication, typically located on a different server and published by a different publisher.

How can I access Wiley InterScience?

Visit http://www.interscience.wiley.com.

Guest Users can browse Wiley InterScience for unrestricted access to journal tables of contents and article abstracts, or use the powerful search engine.

Registered Users are provided with a *Personal Home Page* to store and manage customized alerts, searches, and links to favorite journals and articles. Additionally, Registered Users can view free online sample issues and preview selected material from major reference works.

Licensed Customers are entitled to access full-text journal articles in PDF, with select journals also offering full-text HTML.

How do I become an Authorized User?

Authorized Users are individuals authorized by a paying Customer to have access to the journals in Wiley InterScience. For example, a university that subscribes to Wiley journals is considered to be the Customer. Faculty, staff and students authorized by the university to have access to those journals in Wiley InterScience are Authorized Users. Users should contact their library for information on which Wiley journals they have access to in Wiley InterScience.

ASK YOUR INSTITUTION ABOUT WILEY INTERSCIENCE TODAY!

United States Postal Service

Statement of Ownership, Management, and Circulation

1. Publication Title	2. Publication Number	3. Filing Date
New Directions For Child And Adolescent Development	1 5 2 0 - 3 2 4 7	10/1/04

4. Issue Frequency	5. Number of Issues Published Annually	6. Annual Subscription Price
Quarterly	4	$205.00

7. Complete Mailing Address of Known Office of Publication (Not printer) (Street, city, county, state, and ZIP+4)

Wiley Subscription Services, Inc. at Jossey-Bass, 989 Market Street, San Francisco, CA 94103

Contact Person
Joe Schuman

Telephone
(415) 782-3232

8. Complete Mailing Address of Headquarters or General Business Office of Publisher (Not printer)

Wiley Subscription Services, Inc. 111 River Street, Hoboken, NJ 07030

9. Full Names and Complete Mailing Addresses of Publisher, Editor, and Managing Editor (Do not leave blank)

Publisher (Name and complete mailing address)

Wiley, San Francisco, 989 Market Street, San Francisco, CA 94103-1741

Editor (Name and complete mailing address)

William Damon, Stanford Center On Adolescence, Cypress Bldg., C, Stanford University, Stanford, CA 94305-4145

Managing Editor (Name and complete mailing address)

None

10. Owner (Do not leave blank. If the publication is owned by a corporation, give the name and address of the corporation immediately followed by the names and addresses of all stockholders owning or holding 1 percent or more of the total amount of stock. If not owned by a corporation, give the names and addresses of the individual owners. If owned by a partnership or other unincorporated firm, give its name and address as well as those of each individual owner. If the publication is published by a nonprofit organization, give its name and address.)

Full Name	Complete Mailing Address
Wiley Subscription Services, Inc.	111 River Street, Hoboken, NJ 07030
(see attached list)	

11. Known Bondholders, Mortgagees, and Other Security Holders Owning or Holding 1 Percent or More of Total Amount of Bonds, Mortgages, or Other Securities. If none, check box ▶ ☑ None

Full Name	Complete Mailing Address
None	

12. Tax Status (For completion by nonprofit organizations authorized to mail at nonprofit rates) (Check one)
The purpose, function, and nonprofit status of this organization and the exempt status for federal income tax purposes:
☐ Has Not Changed During Preceding 12 Months
☐ Has Changed During Preceding 12 Months (Publisher must submit explanation of change with this statement)

PS Form 3526, October 1999 (See Instructions on Reverse)

---

13. Publication Title	14. Issue Date for Circulation Data Below
New Directions For Child And Adolescent Development	Summer 2004

15.	Extent and Nature of Circulation	Average No. Copies Each Issue During Preceding 12 Months	No. Copies of Single Issue Published Nearest to Filing Date
a.	Total Number of Copies (Net press run)	990	989
b. Paid and/or Requested Circulation	(1) Paid/Requested Outside-County Mail Subscriptions Stated on Form 3541. (Include advertiser's proof and exchange copies)	283	301
	(2) Paid In-County Subscriptions Stated on Form 3541 (Include advertiser's proof and exchange copies)	0	0
	(3) Sales Through Dealers and Carriers, Street Vendors, Counter Sales, and Other Non-USPS Paid Distribution	0	0
	(4) Other Classes Mailed Through the USPS	0	0
c.	Total Paid and/or Requested Circulation [Sum of 15b. (1), (2),(3),and (4)] ▶	283	301
d. Free Distribution by Mail (Samples, complimentary, and other free)	(1) Outside-County as Stated on Form 3541	0	71
	(2) In-County as Stated on Form 3541	0	0
	(3) Other Classes Mailed Through the USPS	0	0
e.	Free Distribution Outside the Mail (Carriers or other means)	0	0
f.	Total Free Distribution (Sum of 15d. and 15e.) ▶	75	71
g.	Total Distribution (Sum of 15c. and 15f) ▶	358	372
h.	Copies not Distributed	632	617
i.	Total (Sum of 15g. and h.) ▶	990	989
j.	Percent Paid and/or Requested Circulation (15c. divided by 15g. times 100)	79%	81%

16. Publication of Statement of Ownership
☑ Publication required. Will be printed in the Winter 2004 issue of this publication.
☐ Publication not required.

17. Signature and Title of Editor, Publisher, Business Manager, or Owner

Susan E. Lewis, VP & Publisher - Periodicals

Date
10/01/04

I certify that all information furnished on this form is true and complete. I understand that anyone who furnishes false or misleading information on this form or who omits material or information requested on the form may be subject to criminal sanctions (including fines and imprisonment) and/or civil sanctions (including civil penalties).

Instructions to Publishers

1. Complete and file one copy of this form with your postmaster annually on or before October 1. Keep a copy of the completed form for your records.

2. In cases where the stockholder or security holder is a trustee, include in items 10 and 11 the name of the person or corporation for whom the trustee is acting. Also include the names and addresses of individuals who are stockholders who own or hold 1 percent or more of the total amount of bonds, mortgages, or other securities of the publishing corporation. In item 11, if none, check the box. Use blank sheets if more space is required.

3. Be sure to furnish all circulation information called for in item 15. Free circulation must be shown in items 15d, e, and f.

4. Item 15h., Copies not Distributed, must include (1) newsstand copies originally stated on Form 3541, and returned to the publisher, (2) estimated returns from news agents, and (3), copies for office use, leftovers, spoiled, and all other copies not distributed.

5. If the publication had Periodicals authorization as a general or requester publication, this Statement of Ownership, Management, and Circulation must be published; it must be printed in any issue in October or, if the publication is not published during October, the first issue printed after October.

6. In item 16, indicate the date of the issue in which this Statement of Ownership will be published.

7. Item 17 must be signed.

Failure to file or publish a statement of ownership may lead to suspension of Periodicals authorization.

PS Form 3526, October 1999 (Reverse)